OPPOSING
VIEWPOINTS®
SERIES

Natural Disasters

Other Books of Related Interest

Opposing Viewpoints Series

Doomsday Scenarios

At Issue Series

Will the World Run Out of Fresh Water?

Current Controversies Series

Global Warming

"Congress shall make
no law … abridging
the freedom of speech,
or of the press."

First Amendment to the US Constitution

The basic foundation of our democracy is the First Amendment guarantee of freedom of expression. The Opposing Viewpoints Series is dedicated to the concept of this basic freedom and the idea that it is more important to practice it than to enshrine it.

OPPOSING
VIEWPOINTS®
SERIES

Natural Disasters

Margaret Haerens and Lynn M. Zott, Book Editors

GREENHAVEN PRESS
A part of Gale, Cengage Learning

GALE
CENGAGE Learning·

Detroit • New York • San Francisco • New Haven, Conn • Waterville, Maine • London

Elizabeth Des Chenes, *Director, Publishing Solutions*

© 2013 Greenhaven Press, a part of Gale, Cengage Learning

Gale and Greenhaven Press are registered trademarks used herein under license.

For more information, contact:
Greenhaven Press
27500 Drake Rd.
Farmington Hills, MI 48331-3535
Or you can visit our Internet site at gale.cengage.com.

For product information and technology assistance, contact us at:

Gale Customer Support, 1-800-877-4253.
For permission to use material from this text or product, submit all requests online at www.cengage.com/permissions.

Further permissions questions can be emailed to permissionrequest@cengage.com.

Articles in Greenhaven Press anthologies are often edited for length to meet page requirements. In addition, original titles of these works are changed to clearly present the main thesis and to explicitly indicate the author's opinion. Every effort is made to ensure that Greenhaven Press accurately reflects the original intent of the authors. Every effort has been made to trace the owners of copyrighted material.

Cover image © Caitlin Mirra/Shutterstock.com.

LIBRARY OF CONGRESS CATALOGING-IN-PUBLICATION DATA

Natural disasters / Margaret Haerens and Lynn M. Zott, book editors.
    p. cm. -- (Opposing viewpoints)
  Includes bibliographical references and index.
  ISBN 978-0-7377-6060-6 (hardcover) -- ISBN 978-0-7377-6061-3 (pbk.)
  1. Natural disasters. 2. Disaster relief. I. Haerens, Margaret. II. Zott, Lynn M. (Lynn Marie), 1969-
  GB5014.N374 2013
  363.34--dc23

                    2012038616

Printed in the United States of America
1 2 3 4 5   17 16 15 14 13

Contents

Chapter 3: What Should Be the Government's Role in Natural Disaster Relief?

Chapter 4: What Issues Surround the Media's Coverage of Natural Disasters?

Why Consider Opposing Viewpoints?

> "The only way in which a human being
> can make some approach to knowing
> the whole of a subject is by hearing
> what can be said about it by persons of
> every variety of opinion and studying
> all modes in which it can be looked at
> by every character of mind. No wise
> man ever acquired his wisdom in any
> mode but this."
>
> John Stuart Mill

In our media-intensive culture it is not difficult to find differing opinions. Thousands of newspapers and magazines and dozens of radio and television talk shows resound with differing points of view. The difficulty lies in deciding which opinion to agree with and which "experts" seem the most credible. The more inundated we become with differing opinions and claims, the more essential it is to hone critical reading and thinking skills to evaluate these ideas. Opposing Viewpoints books address this problem directly by presenting stimulating debates that can be used to enhance and teach these skills. The varied opinions contained in each book examine many different aspects of a single issue. While examining these conveniently edited opposing views, readers can develop critical thinking skills such as the ability to compare and contrast authors' credibility, facts, argumentation styles, use of persuasive techniques, and other stylistic tools. In short, the Opposing Viewpoints Series is an ideal way to attain the higher-level thinking and reading skills so essential in a culture of diverse and contradictory opinions.

In addition to providing a tool for critical thinking, Opposing Viewpoints books challenge readers to question their own strongly held opinions and assumptions. Most people form their opinions on the basis of upbringing, peer pressure, and personal, cultural, or professional bias. By reading carefully balanced opposing views, readers must directly confront new ideas as well as the opinions of those with whom they disagree. This is not to argue simplistically that everyone who reads opposing views will—or should—change his or her opinion. Instead, the series enhances readers' understanding of their own views by encouraging confrontation with opposing ideas. Careful examination of others' views can lead to the readers' understanding of the logical inconsistencies in their own opinions, perspective on why they hold an opinion, and the consideration of the possibility that their opinion requires further evaluation.

Evaluating Other Opinions

To ensure that this type of examination occurs, Opposing Viewpoints books present all types of opinions. Prominent spokespeople on different sides of each issue as well as well-known professionals from many disciplines challenge the reader. An additional goal of the series is to provide a forum for other, less known, or even unpopular viewpoints. The opinion of an ordinary person who has had to make the decision to cut off life support from a terminally ill relative, for example, may be just as valuable and provide just as much insight as a medical ethicist's professional opinion. The editors have two additional purposes in including these less known views. One, the editors encourage readers to respect others' opinions—even when not enhanced by professional credibility. It is only by reading or listening to and objectively evaluating others' ideas that one can determine whether they are worthy of consideration. Two, the inclusion of such viewpoints encourages the important critical thinking skill of objectively evaluating an author's credentials and bias. This evaluation will illuminate an author's reasons for taking a particular stance on an issue and will aid in readers' evaluation of the author's ideas.

It is our hope that these books will give readers a deeper understanding of the issues debated and an appreciation of the complexity of even seemingly simple issues when good and honest people disagree. This awareness is particularly important in a democratic society such as ours in which people enter into public debate to determine the common good. Those with whom one disagrees should not be regarded as enemies but rather as people whose views deserve careful examination and may shed light on one's own.

Thomas Jefferson once said that "difference of opinion leads to inquiry, and inquiry to truth." Jefferson, a broadly educated man, argued that "if a nation expects to be ignorant and free . . . it expects what never was and never will be." As individuals and as a nation, it is imperative that we consider the opinions of others and examine them with skill and discernment. The Opposing Viewpoints Series is intended to help readers achieve this goal.

David L. Bender and Bruno Leone,
Founders

Introduction

> *"Responding to natural disasters has traditionally been seen as a compassionate response to people in need. While compassion remains at the core of humanitarian action, relief agencies are increasingly conscious of the fact that assistance is rarely neutral and that their actions can have long-term consequences, as evidenced by the 2004 tsunamis in Asia, Hurricane Katrina in 2005, and the earthquake this year [2010] in Haiti."*
>
> *—Elizabeth Ferris, the Brookings Institution*

On January 12, 2010, a massive earthquake hit the small Caribbean country of Haiti. The quake caused major damage to the cities of Port-au-Prince and Jacmel, toppling poorly constructed buildings and ripping apart roads and other infrastructure. It is estimated that more than 3 million people were affected, with thousands of people killed instantly by collapsing buildings and falling debris and thousands more trapped under tons of rubble. Once the initial quake subsided, there were several strong aftershocks across the region, which caused more damage and disrupted rescue efforts. Law enforcement and search-and-rescue teams did the best they could to rescue survivors, but in many cases it was left up to civilians to try to rescue people trapped in collapsed structures. Survivors slept on the streets, afraid that the damaged buildings still standing would be brought down by aftershocks or collapse from damage. Families were torn apart, with many children left orphaned and homeless. Those people left alive had little or no clean water, proper sanitation, food, or medical supplies with which to survive. It is estimated by government officials that around 316,000 people died during the earthquake and its aftermath. That makes the 2010 earthquake in Haiti one of the deadliest earthquakes in recorded history.

As the catastrophic events in Haiti unfolded, thousands of people around the world responded. There was a huge outpouring of financial assistance, with individuals reaching into their pockets and giving to aid organizations of every kind. Donor countries pledged $11 billion for Haiti's recovery and rebuilding.

The money was put to immediate use. Nongovernmental organizations (NGOs) set up humanitarian camps for the displaced, provided tents and food aid, repaired infrastructure, offered medical assistance, reunited families, and perfomed a number of other services. US Marines were deployed to the quake-ravaged country to deliver humanitarian aid and provide security, in conjunction with a larger international effort led by the United Nations. At the airport, disaster aid flowed in from the United States, Brazil, Mexico, Canada, France, Colombia, the Dominican Republic, England, and many other nations. It was a truly international relief effort.

As a neighbor and political and economic superpower, the United States recognized its unique responsibility to help. President Barack Obama underscored the US role in a speech given a few days after the earthquake:

> As the international community continues to respond, I do believe that America has a continued responsibility to act. Our nation has a unique capacity to reach out quickly and broadly and to deliver assistance that can save lives.
>
> That responsibility obviously is magnified when the devastation that's been suffered is so near to us. Haitians are our neighbors in the Americas, and for Americans they are family

and friends. It's characteristic of the American people to help others in time of such severe need. That's the spirit that we will need to sustain this effort as it goes forward. There are going to be many difficult days ahead.

In the days after the quake it seemed that the entire world mobilized to help Haiti rebuild and recover. However, a year later, journalists began to assess the international effort as a failure.

They found that more than a million displaced Haitians were still living in flimsy tents in aid camps or temporary settlements. There was still limited access to clean water and proper sanitation. Unemployment and destitution were rampant. Human trafficking had skyrocketed, and criminal acts were commonplace. A cholera outbreak—which could have been prevented—killed nearly 2,500 people. Only a small fraction of the rubble that clogged streets and hampered rebuilding efforts in Port-au-Prince had been removed.

Despite billions of dollars in aid, tens of thousands of aid workers on the ground, and the combined resources of the United Nations, US military, experienced and well-funded NGOs, and dozens of wealthy donor countries, little progress had been made for the people of Haiti. What had gone wrong?

For analysts, that question had no simple answer. Many blamed international relief organizations for spending funds inefficiently; it was revealed that only about 10 percent of the funds committed to recovery efforts were spent on the ground in Haiti. Money earmarked for rebuilding projects went to foreign corporations instead of Haitian companies, which would have benefited the nation's economy and provided much-needed jobs. NGOs were also accused of fostering a culture of dependence. One Haitian official charged aid organizations with infantilizing the Haitian people and urged NGOs to leave the government to do its job. Other criticisms of NGOs included incompetence, corruption, and widespread bias in the delivery of humanitarian aid.

The Haitian government was also blamed for a weak and ineffective response. Many key government buildings had been destroyed or severely damaged. Government officials had been killed. Before the earthquake, international observers had criticized the political culture in Haiti as largely ineffectual and rife with corruption; they argued that these existing problems had only been exacerbated in the quake's aftermath. For many, it was hard to expect the government to take the lead in rebuilding Haiti when it could not effectively lead before the quake.

The challenges and failures of the Haitian relief effort reflect the larger debate in foreign policy circles about the complicated relationship between aid and development. The authors of the viewpoints presented in *Opposing Viewpoints: Natural Disasters* explore that debate in the following chapters: What Contributes to the Frequency of Natural Disasters?, What Controversies Surround Disaster Relief Efforts?, What Should Be the Government's Role in Natural Disaster Relief?, and What Issues Surround the Media's Coverage of Natural Disasters? The information in this volume will provide some insight into some of the recent controversies surrounding graphic media coverage of natural disasters, the roles of NGOs, corporations, and government in providing disaster relief, and the impact of global warming on the frequency and intensity of droughts, floods, hurricanes, and other catastrophic events.

CHAPTER 1

What Contributes to the Frequency of Natural Disasters?

Chapter Preface

On January 12, 2010, a 7.0 magnitude earthquake hit the small country of Haiti, situated in the Caribbean. The epicenter of the earthquake was just sixteen miles west of Port-au-Prince, the capital city. The violent shaking of the earth toppled buildings and tore apart infrastructure, killing thousands of people instantly and trapping thousands more under tons of rubble. Aftershocks reverberated through the region, causing more damage and disrupting rescue efforts. Hospitals collapsed and communications systems went offline. Roads were blocked by debris, and emergency services could not reach victims in time. Survivors slept on the streets, afraid that aftershocks would cause still-standing buildings to fall in on them while they were inside.

Countries around the world immediately mobilized and sent humanitarian aid to the beleaguered nation. Engineers, support personnel, doctors and medical teams, and search-and-rescue teams were on the ground quickly, working to save people trapped in the rubble of collapsed buildings. Despite valiant efforts, many of these people died waiting for help. It is estimated by government officials that around 316,000 people died during the earthquake and its aftermath. The 2010 earthquake in Haiti is one of the deadliest earthquakes in recorded history.

A day after the earthquake, the well-known American televangelist Pat Robertson called for prayers for the people of Haiti during a broadcast of his show *The 700 Club* on the Christian Broadcasting Network. While expressing compassion for the people going through such a catastrophic disaster, he went on to offer an explanation for the quake and a series of other unfortunate events that had befallen the country since it had successfully rebelled against French colonizers in the nineteenth century.

"Something happened a long time ago in Haiti, and people might not want to talk about it," Robertson said. "They were under the heel of the French . . . and they got together and swore a pact to the devil. They said, 'We will serve you if you'll get us free from the French.' True story. And the devil said, 'OK, it's a deal.' Ever since, they have been cursed by one thing after another."

Robertson's comments ignited a media firestorm, as critics attacked him for attributing the earthquake to God's wrath on the people of Haiti. Robertson was criticized for being callous toward the Haitians' suffering and misinterpreting Haitian history. Hours after the comments were broadcast, the Christian Broadcasting Network released a statement clarifying that Robertson was not saying that the earthquake was God's wrath on the people of Haiti. However, the controversy over Robertson's words continued to simmer for days.

In an op-ed published on January 15, 2010, on FoxNews.com, Bill Schuler, the pastor of Capital Life Church in Arlington, Virginia, defended the debate over the idea that the Haiti earthquake was God's vengeance on the Haitian people. He wrote that:

> The concept originates in the Old Testament, where in the book of Genesis we read of a worldwide flood that came upon the earth as people turned their backs on God. A similar theme can be found in the book of Exodus as God sends plagues upon Egypt because of the disobedience of the Pharaoh and the enslavement of the Hebrew people. Such biblical accounts—that come on the heels of unspent opportunities to repent—are sobering and lead to the question of whether or not we are experiencing such acts of judgment today.

Yet Schuler would not conclusively say that natural disasters were the result of God's wrath. For if the earthquake in Haiti were God's judgment on the Haitian people, was a tornado in Oklahoma that destroys dozens of homes and churches also God's vengeance? Why does God's wrath affect both believers and nonbelievers, the moral and immoral, the innocent and the debased? Such a question has been a topic of theological debates for centuries.

The controversial debate over God's role in natural disasters is one of the subjects explored in the following chapter, which examines the factors that contribute to the frequency of natural disasters. Other viewpoints in the chapter elucidate the impact of technology and global warming on the frequency and intensity of natural disasters.

*"It's becoming amply clear that a
warming world will, on the whole,
see more extreme weather."*

Global Warming Increases
the Frequency and Severity
of Natural Disasters

Brad Plumer

In the following viewpoint, a journalist asserts that although a recent Intergovernmental Panel on Climate Change study concludes that extreme weather events will be much more common in upcoming years because of global warming, it is still extremely difficult to pinpoint the effect of global warming on specific disasters, such as the 2010 heat wave in Moscow. He assesses current research efforts to answer the challenge, finding that researchers are using new methodological techniques to hone the practice of weather attribution. He contends that this is an important issue because of the emerging legal trend of communities and governments suing polluters for climate-caused natural disasters and extreme weather events. Brad Plumer is an energy and environmental reporter for the Washington Post.

As you read, consider the following questions:

1. What did a recent study in *Nature* find about extra greenhouse gases that humans are putting into the air, according to Plumer?
2. According to Stafan Rahmstorf and Dim Coumou, as cited by the author, how likely was it that Moscow's 2010 heat wave would have never occurred without human-made global warming?
3. What does Peter Stott point out about the number of legal cases filed against polluters in years to come, according to Plumer?

The Intergovernmental Panel on Climate Change [IPCC] has a new report out today [November 18, 2011], concluding that global warming will make heat waves, droughts, floods, and other extreme weather events much more common in the decades to come. (It's less clear how climate change will affect hurricanes and tornadoes.) Already in 2010, the United States saw a record number of natural disasters costing $1 billion or more, and the IPCC is warning us not to be shocked if we see even more destructive weather as the Earth heats up.

Pinpointing Specific Disasters

Yet many climate scientists have been trying to go a step further than the IPCC in recent years. It's one thing, after all, to say that a warming world will "load the dice" and make extreme weather events more likely. But is it possible to pinpoint *specific* disasters that are occurring—say, last year's deadly heat wave in Moscow—and say with confidence that global warming is causing those events? That they're not just freak occurrences? And, if so, could that lead to more climate-related lawsuits in the years to come?

It's a surprisingly tricky question. On the one hand, scientists are quite confident that climate change is now causing an uptick in extreme weather events across very broad areas. A recent study in *Nature*, for instance, found that the extra greenhouse

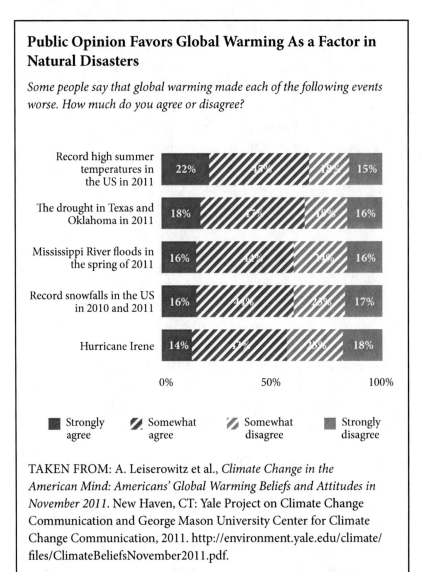

Public Opinion Favors Global Warming As a Factor in Natural Disasters

Some people say that global warming made each of the following events worse. How much do you agree or disagree?

Event	Strongly agree	Somewhat agree	Somewhat disagree	Strongly disagree
Record high summer temperatures in the US in 2011	22%	46%	16%	15%
The drought in Texas and Oklahoma in 2011	18%	47%	18%	16%
Mississippi River floods in the spring of 2011	16%	44%	24%	16%
Record snowfalls in the US in 2010 and 2011	16%	44%	23%	17%
Hurricane Irene	14%	42%	25%	18%

0%   50%   100%

■ Strongly agree   ▨ Somewhat agree   ▨ Somewhat disagree   ■ Strongly disagree

TAKEN FROM: A. Leiserowitz et al., *Climate Change in the American Mind: Americans' Global Warming Beliefs and Attitudes in November 2011.* New Haven, CT: Yale Project on Climate Change Communication and George Mason University Center for Climate Change Communication, 2011. http://environment.yale.edu/climate/ files/ClimateBeliefsNovember2011.pdf.

gases that humans are putting into the air are driving heavier rainfall patterns in the Northern hemisphere. A warmer planet means more water vapor in the atmosphere, which in turn makes storms stronger. Human influence is clear there. But what about *specific* disasters? Is it possible to get that precise?

New Research Demonstrates Likely Relationships

That's what a lot of new research is trying to answer. In October [2011], Stefan Rahmstorf and Dim Coumou published a paper in the *Proceedings of the National Academies of Science* [*PNAS*] that looked at at the 2010 heat wave in Moscow, when temperatures hit record highs and killed hundreds. The researchers examined more than a century of data and used statistical techniques to tease out natural variability from the long-term warming trend. They concluded there was an 80 percent likelihood that Moscow's heat wave would never have occurred without man-made global warming.

"Our study was of a loaded-dice type," Rahmstorf told me. "We're not attributing an individual event to a cause. We're saying that this sort of weather event has become five times more likely." But, he added, "in practice, when you say it's 80 percent likely, then it's very close to a single-event attribution. The dice is loaded so strongly that you can say it's almost certain" that global warming caused the heat wave. The *PNAS* paper introduced a new methodological technique—using what's known as Monte Carlo simulations—to make these sorts of attributions, which opens up new avenues of exploration.

Similarly, a recent peer-reviewed paper by researchers at the National Ocean and Atmospheric Administratiom [NOAA] concluded that climate change was partly responsible for a series of recent wintertime droughts in the Mediterranean region. "The magnitude and frequency of the drying that has occurred is too great to be explained by natural variability alone," said NOAA's Martin Hoerling, the lead author of the study, in a news release.

Challenges Remain

In a phone interview, Hoerling explained the challenges of sorting out just how much blame to assign global warming for any given disaster: "Imagine you have a lot of historical data and you've decided that a heat wave can never get bigger than 9°C," he says. "That's the biggest heat wave possible from natural factors. So then you find that, because of human influences, temperatures have warmed 1°C. And now along comes a 10°C heat wave. You can say that this never would have happened without human influence. But you could also say that 90 percent of it was due to natural variability."

Hoerling notes that it's a lot easier to separate out the climate signal in heat waves, since temperature data is fairly straightforward. It's much harder, however, to assign blame for individual storms, since natural variability for precipitation is stronger and more erratic. "That involves a lot more complexity: how does this storm track, how do changes in ocean temperature factor in?" he said. Even though we know that humans are having an overall influence on precipitation patterns, getting precise is still a challenge.

We're likely to see more climate research along these lines in the future. But why does it matter? As Peter Stott, of UK's Met Office Hadley Center, has pointed out, it's quite possible that we could see more legal suits being brought against polluters for climate-caused natural disasters in the years ahead. In that case, he notes, "there would be a requirement for objective and scientifically robust information" on the causes of specific disasters. The science of weather attribution isn't *quite* at that point yet, but it's progressing rapidly.

Still, even if we can't always assign blame for an isolated disaster, it's becoming amply clear that a warming world will, on the whole, see more extreme weather.

"Many scientists have dismissed the supposed causal relationship between [global warming and natural disasters] for a long time."

The Link Between Global Warming and Natural Disasters Is Based on Bad Science

Rich Trzupek

In the following viewpoint, a writer criticizes the International Panel on Climate Change for employing "shockingly sloppy science" to suggest a link between global warming and the melting of Himalayan glaciers. He views this incident as just one in a pattern of exaggerations and speculation from scientific organizations and groups bent on proving links between global warming and natural disasters and extreme weather. He points out that there have been a number of scientists that have questioned and even dismissed the causal relationship between the two for years. Rich Trzupek is an author and senior environmental adviser to the Heartland Institute.

As you read, consider the following questions:

1. How does Trzupek describe "Climategate"?

2. According to John Coleman and Joseph D'Aleo, as cited by the author, the National Oceanic and Atmospheric Administration has reduced the number of global weather stations it uses by how many?
3. According to a recent Pew survey cited by Trzupek, what percentage of Americans believes that global warming should be a top policy priority?

R ecent history has been unkind to those who maintain that human activity is leading to catastrophic climate change.

Two months ago [in November 2009], we had "Climategate," the scandal that revealed how the University of East Anglia's Climatic Research Unit [CRU] had conspired to manipulate data and to bully scientific publications in order to silence scholarship that failed to affirm the global warming gospel. Last month [December 2009], the failure of the International Panel on Climate Change (IPCC) to reach any kind of meaningful agreement to reduce greenhouse gas emissions dealt another hammer blow to the cause. The latest setback came last week [in January 2010], when the world was presented with a new climate scandal: Glaciergate.

Glaciergate

In the latest case, it turns out that the IPCC employed shockingly sloppy science to suggest that, as a consequence of global warming, Himalayan glaciers were on the verge of destruction. Specifically, the IPCC fabricated a non-existent link between climate change and natural disasters. In its 2007 report, IPCC claimed that:

> Glaciers in the Himalayas are receding faster than in any other part of the world, and if the present rate continues, the likelihood of them disappearing by the year 2035 and perhaps sooner is very high if the Earth keeps warming at the current rate.

That statement, it turns out, was not based so much on science as on speculation. It was based on a report published by the World Wildlife Fund in 2005. That report in turn was based on an article published in *New Scientist* in 1999, which had no scientific grounding at all. Glaciers don't—can't—melt that fast. If the current rate of melting continues, Himalayan glaciers *might* disappear in hundreds of years, not twenty five, which is the kind of "rounding error" that seems to permeate climate science.

A Ridiculous Assertion

The IPCC should have known better than to publish anything so patently ridiculous, and there were plenty of skeptics who told them so. "The absurdity was obvious to anyone who had studied the scientific literature," Patrick J. Michaels, a senior fellow in environmental policy at the libertarian Cato Institute, said. "This was not an honest mistake. IPCC had been warned about it for a year by many scientists."

The chair of the IPCC, railroad engineer Rajendra Pachauri, acknowledged the grievous error in a press release, stating that the report presented:

> poorly substantiated rates of recession and dates for the disappearance of Himalayan glaciers. In drafting the paragraph in question, the clear and well-established standards of evidence, required by the IPCC procedures, were not applied properly.

"Obviously this is an isolated incident," NASA [National Aeronautics and Space Administration] scientist and global warming apologist Gavin Schmidt wrote at his website, realclimate.org. Replace Gavin's "The IPCC Is Not Infallible" header with "The IPCC Is Not Credible" and he might be a bit more believable. The more we learn about the way the IPCC does things, the less reason to entrust the future of the planet to this organization.

More Sloppy Climate Work

Speaking of "isolated incidents," the 2007 IPCC report also said:

> Once the data were normalized, a small statistically significant trend was found for an increase in annual catastrophe loss

Climategate

Things really heated up for [climate scientist Michael] Mann in late 2009, when more than 1,000 emails from him and other climate scientists were lifted from a server at the Climatic Research Unit (CRU) of the UK's University of East Anglia, the world's leading research institution focused on climate change. The emails offered a window into the climate-science bunker, with a view of Mann and his fellow researchers growing increasingly defensive. One scientist wrote that he was "tempted to beat the crap out of" a skeptic at the libertarian Cato Institute. Another joked that the way to deal with skeptics was "continuing to publish quality work in quality journals (or calling in a Mafia hit)." Scientists suggested that they would rather destroy data than provide them to their critics. They also discussed using "tricks" in their research, debated how to frame uncertainties in some of their data, and attempted to control access to peer-reviewed journals.

Within days, the heist—soon dubbed "Climategate"—was all over the news. [Conservative TV commentator] Glenn Beck called it a "potentially major scandal"; Fox News crowed that the emails "undercut the whole scientific claim for man's impact on global warming." Rep. James Sensenbrenner (R-Wis.) decried them as evidence of "scientific fascism."

Kate Sheppard, "The Hackers and the Hockey Stick: Unraveling the Truth Behind Climategate," Mother Jones, May–June 2011.

since 1970 of 2% a year. Once losses are normalized for exposure, there still remains an underlying rising trend.

This statement forms the basis for alarmist claims that global warming is causing more severe weather around the world. We now know that this statement was based on a research paper authored by Robert Muir-Wood of Risk Management Solutions of London, a paper that was not actually finalized until 2008, a year *after* IPCC 2007 was published. And this will come as no surprise: Muir-Wood concluded that there is no linkage between natural disasters like hurricanes, tornados, etc. and "climate change."

Again, many scientists have dismissed the supposed causal relationship between the two for a long time. "All the literature published before and since the IPCC report shows that rising disaster losses can be explained entirely by social change," Roger Pielke, professor of environmental studies at Colorado University, said. "People have looked hard for evidence that global warming plays a part but can't find it. Muir-Wood's study actually confirmed that."

The US Version of Climategate

Which brings us to the United States' very own version of Climategate. Legendary meteorologist John Coleman hosted a special broadcast aired by San Diego television station KUSI last week. According to Coleman and the Weather Channel's Joseph D'Aleo NOAA [National Oceanic and Atmospheric Adminstration] has altered its method of representing global temperatures in order to inflate temperature increases. Coleman and D'Aleo say that NOAA reduced the number of global weather stations it uses from over 7,000 to less than 1,500 in order to artificially inflate temperatures. Consider one telling example from the broadcast: NOAA records temperatures in California based on weather stations in San Francisco and Los Angeles only. Weather stations located in the cooler, more upland regions of the state are no longer part of the data set.

NOAA doesn't see any problems with its methodologies, relying heavily on the techniques developed by NASA's Dr. James Hansen to estimate worldwide temperatures. Of course, the fact that Hansen is one of the nation's most ardent global warming alarmists makes one wonder why anyone would entrust him with the task of proving a theory he has already declared to be irrefutable. According to the NOAA:

> The analysis method was documented in Hansen and Lebedeff (1987), showing that the correlation of temperature change was reasonably strong for stations separated by up to 1200 km, especially at middle and high latitudes.

"Reasonably strong?" Not exactly a ringing endorsement. Nor does NOAA explain why, when trying to take the temperature of an entire planet, less data is better than more. It all strikes this scientist as very suspicious. But then this is the same NOAA that has simultaneously claimed that 2009 is one of the warmest years on record and that the summer of 2009 is the 34th coolest season recorded. The CRU scandal; disappearing glaciers that remain stubbornly in place; relying on research that doesn't actually exist; more fun and games with temperature data—how many more blows can the alarmists take?

Fraudulent Theory

Three years ago [in 2007], thirty-eight percent of Americans thought that global warming should be a top policy priority. The most recent Pew survey now pegs the number at twenty-eight percent. Himalayan glaciers won't disappear in the next twenty-five years, but when the more fragile science upon which global warming theory is built comes to light, significant public support for alarmism may melt away in a tenth of the time.

"Every bit of carbon we keep out of the atmosphere is that much less . . . disaster waiting to happen."

Humans Have a Responsibility to Reduce Carbon Emissions That Contribute to Natural Disasters

Bill McKibben

In the following viewpoint, a journalist contends that the earth is entering a new geological epoch called the Anthropocene, which is characterized by higher levels of carbon dioxide near the planet's surface, warmer temperatures, moister air, and more frequent and destructive natural disasters and extreme weather events. He suggests that these changes are largely caused by humanity's consumerism and greed, which over the decades have served to remake the planet. He urges people to become more environmentally responsible and reduce carbon emissions in order to prevent more natural disasters and extreme weather in the years ahead. Bill McKibben is an author and environmentalist.

Bill McKibben, "Natural Disasters?," *Guardian*, April 1, 2011. Copyright © 2011 by the Guardian. All rights reserved. Reproduced by permission.

As you read, consider the following questions:

1. Why does the author believe that the Holocene Era was an excellent time to build a civilization?
2. How much moister is the atmosphere than it was just a few decades ago, according to McKibben?
3. According to a recent poll read by McKibben, what did the majority of Americans say most likely caused natural disasters: climate change or God's displeasure?

A t least since Noah, and likely long before, we've stared in horror at catastrophe and tried to suss out deeper meaning—it was but weeks ago that the Tokyo governor, Shintaro Ishihara, declared that the [March 2011] earthquake/tsunami/reactor tripleheader was "divine punishment" for excess consumerism. This line of reasoning usually fails to persuade these days (why are Las Vegas and Dubai unscathed by anything except the housing meltdown?) but it's persistent. We need *some* explanation for why our stable world is suddenly cracked in half or under water. Still, over time we've become less superstitious, since science can explain these cataclysms. Angry gods or plate tectonics? We're definitely moving towards natural explanation of crises.

Which is odd, because the physical world is moving in the other direction.

The Holocene Era

The Holocene—the 10,000 years through which we have just come—was by all accounts a period of calm and stability on Earth. Temperatures and sea levels were relatively stable. Hence it was an excellent time to build a civilisation, especially the modern kind that comes with lots of stuff: roads, buildings, container ports, nuclear reactors. Yes, we had disasters throughout those millennia, some of them ([the eruption of the Indonesian volcano] Krakatoa, say) simply enormous. Hurricanes blew, earthquakes rocked. But they were, by definition, rare, taking us by surprise—freaks, outliers, traumas that persisted in our collective history precisely because they were so unusual.

A New Era

We're now moving into a new geological epoch, one scientists are calling the Anthropocene—a world remade by man, most obvious in his emissions of carbon dioxide. That CO_2 traps heat near the planet that would otherwise have radiated back to space—there is, simply, more energy in our atmosphere than there used to be. And that energy expresses itself in many ways: ice melts, water heats, clouds gather. 2010 was the warmest year on record, and according to insurers—the people we task with totting up disasters—it demonstrated the unprecedented mayhem this new heat causes. Global warming was "the only plausible explanation", the giant reinsurer Munich Re explained in December, of 2010's catastrophes, the drought, heatwave and fires across Russia, and the mega-floods in Pakistan, Australia, Brazil and elsewhere were at least plausibly connected to the general heating. They were, that is to say, not precisely "natural disasters", but something more complex; the human thumb was on the scale.

We still have plenty of purely natural disasters—though scientists can posit reasons climate change might make the world more seismically active, tectonic and volcanic forces seem beyond our reach; the great wave that broke over Sendai really did come out of the blue. But even in Japan, of course, the disaster was not entirely "natural". The subsequent fallout was . . . fallout, the invisible plume streaming from one of our highest-tech marvels, a complex reduced in minutes into something almost elemental, a kind of utility-owned volcano.

In a sense Ishihara was correct when he decried "selfish greed". It is consumerism that has flooded the atmosphere with CO_2: the constant getting and spending, where \$1 spent liberates roughly 1 lb of carbon. We are remaking the world, and quickly; we are stumbling into a new way of thinking about disaster, where neither God nor nature but man is to blame.

"Climate Change Is a Hoax," cartoon by Paul Fell. www.CartoonStock.com.

The Consequences of Global Warming

That changes the valence of catastrophe. Since warm air holds more water vapour than cold, the atmosphere is nearly 5% moister than it was just a few decades ago. That loads the dice for great floods of the kind suddenly so common. I lived through one in my small mountain town in Vermont two summers ago: the biggest thunderstorm in our history dropped buckets of rain in a matter of hours. Our town is almost entirely intact forest; it should have been able to hold whatever nature threw at it. But that rain fell on a different planet from the one the forest had grown up on; every road washed out, and the governor had to visit by helicopter. But at least we had the solace (or self-lacerating realisation) that we'd helped cause this deep change. Americans burn more carbon per capita than just about anyone; what do you say to a Pakistani farmer watching the swollen Indus wash away his life's work? And since global warming seems to take first aim at the poorest places that have done the least to cause it, this is a question we may be asking ourselves a good deal in the decades to come.

Not every natural disaster is unnatural now, and we may be able to fool ourselves a little longer. But these days it's the climate deniers who act like the pious of yore, unable to accept the truth. I was surprised, and impressed, to read a poll of Americans taken recently. By healthy majorities, this most religious of western citizenries said natural disasters were more likely to be a sign of climate change than of God's displeasure.

Which is good news, because for the first time in human history we can prevent a great deal of unnecessary cataclysm in the years ahead. Not all of it—there will always be earthquakes and hurricanes. But every bit of carbon we keep out of the atmosphere is that much less extra energy we add to the system. It's that much less disaster waiting to happen.

> *"We have built vast networks of technology [that are] . . . vulnerable to catastrophic disasters . . . [but] technology also mitigates disasters."*

Technology Can Both Create Natural Disasters and Aid in Disaster Recovery

Joel Achenbach

In the following viewpoint, a writer predicts that this century will be full of natural disasters and technological crises and "unholy combinations of the two." He contends that humans have succeeded in reengineering the planet and creating interconnected technological networks that improve day-to-day life immensely but can exacerbate and even cause catastrophic events. He also argues that it is clear that climate change will function to intensify natural disasters in the next decades, creating more uncertainty and devastation. It is imperative, he concludes, that international, national, regional, and local governments, as well as communities and families, develop strategies to better prevent and survive catastrophic natural and technological disasters. Joel Achenbach is an author and reporter for the Washington Post.

As you read, consider the following questions:
1. What is an ARkStorm, according to Achenbach?
2. How many cities does the author say have at least 1 million people?
3. According to Achenbach, how did technology help save lives during the deadly storms of April 27, 2011?

This will be the century of disasters.

In the same way that the 20th century was the century of world wars, genocide, and grinding ideological conflict, the 21st will be the century of natural disasters and technological crises and unholy combinations of the two. It'll be the century when the things that we count on to go right will, for whatever reason, go wrong.

A Plethora of Dangers

Late last month [April 2011], as the Mississippi River rose in what is destined to be the worst flood in decades, and as the residents of Alabama and other states rummaged through the debris of a historic tornado outbreak, physicists at a meeting in Anaheim, Calif., had a discussion about the dangers posed by the sun.

Solar flares, scientists believe, are a disaster waiting to happen. Thus one of the sessions at the American Physical Society's annual meeting was devoted to discussing the hazard of electromagnetic pulses (EMPs) caused by solar flares or terrorist attacks. Such pulses could fry transformers and knock out the electrical grid over much of the nation. Last year the Oak Ridge National Laboratory released a study saying the damage might take years to fix and cost trillions of dollars.

But maybe even that's not the disaster people should be worrying about. Maybe they should worry instead about the ARkStorm. That's the name the U.S. Geological Survey [USGS]'s Multihazards Demonstration Project gave to a hypothetical storm that would essentially turn much of California's Central Valley into a bathtub. It has happened before, in 1861–62, when it rained for 45 straight days. The USGS explains: "The ARkStorm draws heat and moisture from the tropical Pacific, forming a series of Atmospheric Rivers (ARs) that approach the ferocity of hurricanes and then slam into the U.S. West Coast over several weeks." The result, the USGS determined, could be a flood that would cost $725 billion in direct property losses and economic impact.

While pondering this, don't forget the Cascadia subduction zone. That's the plate boundary off the coast of the Pacific Northwest, one that could generate a tsunami much like the one that devastated Japan in March [2011]. The Cascadia subduction zone runs from Vancouver Island to northern California, and last ruptured in a major tsunami-spawning earthquake on January 26, 1700. It could break at any moment, with catastrophic consequences.

"Black Swan" Events

All of these things have the common feature of low probability and high consequence. They're "black swan" events. They're unpredictable in any practical sense. They're also things that ordinary people probably should not worry about on a daily basis. You can't fear the sun. You can't worry that a rock will fall out of the sky and smash the earth, or that the ground will open up and swallow you like a vitamin. A key element of maintaining one's sanity is knowing how to ignore risks that are highly improbable at any given point in time.

And yet in the coming century, these or other black swans will seem to occur with surprising frequency. There are several reasons for this. We have chosen to engineer the planet. We have built vast networks of technology. We have created systems that, in general, work very well, but are still vulnerable to catastrophic failures. It is harder and harder for any one person, institution, or agency to perceive all the interconnected elements of the technological society. Failures can cascade. There are unseen weak points in the network. Small failures can have broad consequences.

Most importantly: We have more people, and more stuff, standing in the way of calamity. We're not suddenly having more earthquakes, but there are now 7 billion of us, a majority living in cities. In 1800, only Beijing could count a million inhabitants, but at last count there were 381 cities with at least 1 million people. Many are "megacities" in seismically hazardous places—Mexico City, Caracas, Tehran, and Kathmandu being among those with a lethal combination of weak infrastructure (unreinforced masonry buildings) and a shaky foundation.

The Role of Technology

Natural disasters will increasingly be accompanied by technological crises—and the other way around. In March, the Japan earthquake triggered the Fukushima Daiichi nuclear power plant meltdown. Last year, a technological failure on the Deepwater Horizon drilling rig in the Gulf of Mexico led to the environmental crisis of the oil spill. . . .

In both the Deepwater Horizon and Fukushima disasters, the safety systems weren't nearly as robust as the industries believed. In these technological accidents, there are hidden pathways for the gremlins to infiltrate the operation. In the case of Deepwater Horizon, a series of decisions by BP and its contractors led to a loss of well control—the initial blowout. The massive blowout preventer on the sea floor was equipped with a pair of pinchers known as blind shear rams. They were supposed to cut the drill-pipe and shear the well. The forensic investigation indicated that the initial eruption of gas buckled the pipe and prevented the blind shear rams from getting a clean bite on it. So the "backup" plan—cut the pipe—was effectively eliminated in the initial event, the loss of well control.

Fukushima also had a backup plan that wasn't far enough back. The nuclear power plant had backup generators in case the grid went down. But the generators were on low ground, and were blasted by the tsunami. Without electricity, the power company had no way to cool the nuclear fuel rods. In a sense, it

The California Storms of 1861–1862

Beginning in early December 1861 and continuing into early 1862, an extreme series of storms lasting 45 days struck California. The storms caused severe flooding, turning the Sacramento Valley into an inland sea, forcing the state capitol to be moved temporarily from Sacramento to San Francisco, and requiring Governor Leland Stanford to take a rowboat to his inauguration. William Brewer, author of "*Up and Down California*," wrote on January 19, 1862, "The great central valley of the state is under water—the Sacramento and San Joaquin valleys—a region 250 to 300 miles long and an average of at least twenty miles wide, or probably three to three and a half millions of acres!"

The 1861–62 series of storms were the largest and longest California storms in the historic record, but were probably not the worst California has experienced. Geological evidence indicates that floods that occurred before Europeans arrived were bigger. Scientists looking at the thickness of sediment layers collected offshore in the Santa Barbara and San Francisco Bay areas have found geologic evidence of megastorms that occurred in the years 212, 440, 603, 1029, 1418, and 1605. . . . There is no scientific evidence to suggest that such extreme storms could not happen again.

Keith Porter et al., "Overview of the
ARkStorm Scenario," US Geological Survey,
Open File Report 2010-1312, 2011.

was a very simple problem: a power outage. Some modern reactors coming online have passive cooling systems for backups—they rely on gravity and evaporation to circulate the cooling water.

Charles Perrow, author of *Normal Accidents,* told me that computer infrastructure is a disaster in the making. "Watch out for failures in cloud computing," he said by email. "They will have consequences for medical monitoring systems and much else."

The Positive Effect of Technology

Technology also mitigates disasters, of course. Pandemics remain a threat, but modern medicine can help us stay a step ahead of evolving microbes. Satellites and computer models helped meteorologists anticipate the deadly storms of April 27 [2011] and warn people to find cover in advance of the twisters. Better building codes save lives in earthquakes. Chile, which has strict building codes, was hit with a powerful earthquake last year [2010] but suffered only a fraction of the fatalities and damage that impoverished Haiti endured just weeks earlier.

The current Mississippi flood is an example of technology at work for better and for worse. As I write, the Army Corps of Engineers is poised to open the Morganza spillway and flood much of the Atchafalaya basin. That's not a "disaster" but a solution of sorts, since the alternative is the flooding of cities downstream and possible levee failure. Of course, the levees might still fail. We'll see. But this is how the system is supposed to work.

On the other hand, the broader drainage system of the Mississippi River watershed is set up in a way that it makes floods more likely. The cornfields in parts of the upper Midwest, for example, have been "tiled" with pipes that carry excess rainwater rapidly to the rip-rapped streams and on down to rivers lined with levees. We gave up natural drainage decades ago. The Mississippi is like a catheter at this point. Had nature remained in charge, the river would have mitigated much of its downstream flooding by spreading into natural floodplains further upriver (and the main channel would have long ago switched to the Atchafalaya river basin—see John McPhee's *The Control of Nature*—and New Orleans would no longer be a riverfront city).

Risks Cannot Be Engineered Away

One wild card for how disastrous this century will become is climate change. There's been a robust debate on the blogs about whether the recent weather events (tornadoes, floods) can be attributed to climate change. It's a briar patch of an issue and I'll exercise my right to skip past it for the most part. But I think it's clear that climate change will exacerbate natural disasters in general in coming years, and introduce a new element of risk and uncertainty into a future in which we have plenty of risks and uncertainties already. This, we don't need.

And by the way: Any discussion of "geoengineering" as a solution to climate change needs to be examined with the understanding that engineering systems can and *will* fail. You don't want to bet the future of the planet on an elaborate technological fix in which everything has to work perfectly. If failure isn't an option, maybe you shouldn't try it to begin with.

So if we can't engineer our way out of our engineered disasters, and if natural disasters are going to keep pummeling us as they have since the dawn of time—what's our strategy? Other than, you know, despair?

Formulating a Strategy

Well, that's always worked for me, but here are a few more practical thoughts to throw in the mix. First, we might want to try some regulation by people with no skin in the game. That might mean, for example, government regulators who make as much money as the people they're regulating. Or it could even mean a private-sector regulatory apparatus that polices the industry, cracking down on rogue operators. The point is, we don't want every risky decision made by people with pecuniary interests.

Second, we need to keep things in perspective: The apparent onslaught of disasters doesn't portend the end of the world. Beware disaster hysteria in the news media. The serial disasters of the 21st century will be, to some extent, a matter of perception. It'll feel like we're bouncing from disaster to disaster in part because of the shrinking of the world and the ubiquity of communications technology. [News reporters] Anderson Cooper and Sanjay Gupta are always in a disaster zone somewhere, demanding to know why the cavalry hasn't showed up.

Third, we should think in terms of how we can boost our societal "resilience." This is the buzzword in the disaster-preparedness industry. Think of what you would do, and what your community would do, after a disaster. You can't always dodge the disaster, but perhaps you can still figure out how to recover quickly. How would we communicate if we got flared by the sun and the grid went down over two-thirds of the country? How would we even know what was going on? Maybe we need to have the occasional "18th-century weekend" to see how people might get through a couple of days without the grid, the cell towers, the cable TV, the iTunes downloads—the full Hobbesian nightmare.[1]

And make an emergency plan. Buy some batteries and jugs of water just for starters. Figure out how the things around you work. Learn about your community infrastructure. Read about science, technology, and engineering, and don't worry if you don't understand all the jargon. And then, having done that, go on about your lives, pursuing happiness on a planet that, though sometimes dangerous, is by far the best one we've got.

Note

1. Seventeenth-century philosopher Thomas Hobbes reasoned that life without civil society would be "solitary, poor, nasty, brutish, and short."

"The desire to turn to God for an explanation after a disaster is a widespread human urge."

Many Americans Believe That God Causes Natural Disasters

Stephanie Pappas

In the following viewpoint, the author reports that recent public opinion polls show that a majority of Americans believe that God is in control of everything that happens on earth and that slightly fewer blame God for inflicting natural disasters on the planet. She interviews experts who suggest that people turn to God for a comforting sense of order and stability following horrible events, such as the 2011 earthquake and tsunami in Japan. Americans who interpret the Bible more literally are more likely to attribute natural disasters to God's hand, according to her report. Stephanie Pappas is a senior writer at the LiveScience website.

As you read, consider the following questions:

1. According to a recent poll cited by Pappas, what percentage of Americans agree or mostly agree that God is in control of all earthly events?

2. What percentage of Americans does the author cite as believing in a vengeful God?
3. What percentage of white evangelicals believe that God sometimes punishes entire nations for the sins of a few, according to the poll cited by Pappas?

According to just over half of Americans, God is in control of everything that happens on Earth. But slightly fewer are willing to blame an omnipotent power for natural disasters such as Japan's earthquake and tsunami.

A new poll finds that 56 percent of Americans agree or mostly agree that God is in control of all Earthly events. Forty-four percent think that natural disasters are or could be a sign from the Almighty. The fire-and-brimstone version of a vengeful God is even less popular in America: Only 29 percent of people felt that God sometimes punishes an entire nation for the sins of a few individuals.

Nonetheless, the desire to turn to God for an explanation after a disaster is a widespread human urge, said Scott Schieman, a sociologist at the University of Toronto who studies people's beliefs about God's influence on daily life.

"There's just something about the randomness of the universe that is too unsettling," Schieman told LiveScience. "We like explanations for why things happen . . . many times people weave in these divine narratives."

Deity of Disaster

The poll surveyed a random sample of 1,008 adults in the continental United States in the few days after the Japanese disaster. The sample was weighted by age, sex, geographic region, education and race to reflect the entire population of U.S. adults.

The poll found that evangelical Christians are more likely to see disasters as a sign from God than other religious faiths. Of white evangelicals, 59 percent said disasters are or could be a message from the deity, compared with 31 percent of Catholics and 34 percent of non-evangelical Protestants. The margin of error for the survey was plus or minus 3 percent.

Forty-four percent of all Americans said that recent natural disasters could be a sign of the Biblical end times, with 67 percent of white evangelicals holding that view. (In comparison, 58 percent of Americans attributed recent severe natural disasters to global climate change, as did 52 percent of evangelicals.)

It makes sense that those who interpret the Bible more literally would link disasters to God, said David Foy, a psychologist at Pepperdine University in Los Angeles who has studied religious coping and post-traumatic stress disorder. However, Foy said, the poll should be interpreted with caution.

"They try to draw some conclusions between evangelicals and mainline Protestants and Catholics, and I don't think they can do that from the data that they've got," Foy told LiveScience. "[The poll participants] weren't selected on those variables, and other things that could have influenced their responses weren't controlled."

A Vengeful God?

The poll found that 53 percent of white evangelical respondents and 20 percent of Catholics and mainline protestants said God sometimes punishes entire nations for the sins of a few.

That belief can make it harder to cope after a tragedy, Foy said. In his work with combat veterans, Foy has found that those who see tragedies as evidence of God's wrath are not as psychologically well-off as those who seek other explanations for negative events.

Less clear are the risks and benefits of believing that God is in the driver's seat, Schieman said, adding that the number of people in the survey who believe in a God that controls the universe (56 percent) matches what he's seen in his work.

"It doesn't surprise me, especially given the nature of God-talk in everyday society, how people talk about God being in control and influential," he said.

Among the group of people who believe in a take-charge kind of God are those who see the hand in the divine in every aspect of life, down to the number of empty parking spaces at a busy shopping mall, Schieman said. And then there are those who see God as an absentee sort of manager—someone who cares and is in-charge, but isn't fiddling with the weather or engineering tsunamis.

"It's an interesting question," Schieman said. "If you package or interpret events like this in the context of divine control, does it make people feel better? Does it make people feel more motivated?"

No Straightforward Answer

There's no straightforward answer to that question, Schieman said. In one 2008 study of data from a phone survey of U.S. adults, Schieman found that people who believed in a controlling God felt that they had less personal control over their own lives. But that association was strongest in people who rarely prayed or went to religious services. Those who believed in a controlling God but were invested in services and prayer showed no decrease in personal feelings of control, Schieman found.

One of the toughest questions for believers is how to reconcile the image of an "all-powerful, all-good and all-mighty" deity with one that allows disasters like the Japanese tsunami, Foy said. How people cope with the question depends on their conception of God, he said.

"If you believe God ultimately is in charge of everything but doesn't control the minutiae of daily life, then I think it's easier to reconcile," Foy said. "God would still care, but did not cause the tsunami to punish people."

> *"Few Americans think natural disasters are signs from God and . . . even fewer believe God punishes nations for the sins of its citizens."*

Most Americans Do Not Believe That God Causes Natural Disasters

Eric Marrapodi

In the following viewpoint, a journalist points out that although a majority of Americans surveyed in a new Public Religion Research Institute poll believe that God is responsible for everything that happens in the world, significantly fewer attribute natural disasters to God or God's vengeance on a sinful populace. The author reports that a number of factors influenced the way people answered the pollsters, including a respondent's religion, place of worship, political views, and perception of the Bible. Some, according to the author, contend that there is general reluctance to think of God as vengeful, and people tend to look for other explanations for horrible disasters. Eric Marrapodi is coeditor of the CNN Belief Blog.

As you read, consider the following questions:
1. According to a recent survey conducted by the Public Religion Research Institute and cited by Marrapodi, what percentage of Americans believe that earthquakes, floods, and other natural disasters are a sign from God?
2. What percentage of Americans attributed the increased severity of natural disasters to global warming, according to the author?
3. What percentage of respondents to the Public Religion Research Institute poll cited by Marrapodi believe that it was very important or somewhat important to financially assist the victims of the Japanese earthquake and tsunami?

A new survey conducted on the heels of Japan's devastating earthquake and tsunami finds that few Americans think natural disasters are signs from God and that even fewer believe God punishes nations for the sins of its citizens, as some suggested after the Japanese disaster.

At the same time, most Americans believe God is responsible for everything that happens in the world, according to the survey. . . .

The survey was conducted by the Public Religion Research Institute in partnership with the Religion News Service.

Differing Beliefs in Divine Punishment

Fewer than 4 in 10 Americans (38%) believe that earthquakes, floods and other natural disasters are a sign from God, while roughly 3 in 10 believe that God sometimes punishes nations for the sins of some citizens, according to the survey.

A majority of people who self-identified as white evangelical Christians bucked the consensus against God punishing nations for the sins of its citizens, with 53% saying they believed that to be true.

Even more white evangelicals—59%—believe that natural disasters are a sign from God, while only about one-third of Catholics and white mainline Protestants share that view.

Two thirds of white evangelicals also believe that natural disasters are evidence of the "end times," according to the survey.

The survey was conducted by telephone with 1,008 adults in the continental United States between March 17–20 [2011] as news was pouring in from the hardest-hit areas in Japan.

The margin of error for the survey is plus or minus 3 percentage points.

Poll Results Show a Variety of Beliefs

Fifty-six percent of all respondents said they believe God is in control of everything that happens in the world, according to the poll.

And 7 in 10 Americans believe God is a person with whom a person can have a relationship, according to the poll.

But most Americans—58%—said they attributed the increased severity of natural disasters to global warming, while 44% said they attribute it to what the Bible sometimes refers to as the "end times."

The respondents tended to split along party lines—52% of Republicans said the increased severity could be attributed to "end times" prophecies, while 75% of Democrats said it was the result of global warming.

"These kind of questions about God being in control and there simultaneously being suffering are the kind of things that keep seminarians up at night. They're thorny theological issues. We wanted to see if we could get at it with polling to see what Americans think," pollster Robert P. Jones, CEO of the Public Religion Research Institute, told CNN.

"We asked people how many were following what was going on in Japan, and nine out of 10 said they had heard a lot. This is something very clearly on the minds of Americans as they answered this poll."

God Does Not Punish with Tragedy

God does not cause natural disasters to punish us any more than God wills a child to be hit by a drunk driver.

God does not flood river banks to show us God's strength. . . . God doesn't kill people to teach us a lesson.

Emily C. Heath, "God Doesn't Cause Natural Disasters to Punish Us," The Commons, no. #117, September 7, 2011. www.commonsnews.org.

Many Factors Influence Poll Results

Jones said that where respondents worship played a big role in how they answered the questions.

"One thing that may be underlying this is how one approaches the Bible. Evangelical white Protestants are much more likely to take a literal approach to the Bible. In the Bible, natural disasters are used as a sign or as a punishment from God. Mainline Protestants and Catholics have a much less literal view of the bible," Jones said.

Regardless of which pew American Christians find themselves in during the weekend, their beliefs about God's role in matters like this are something Jones says brings a lot of debate.

Ryan Coyne, a philosopher of religion at the University of Chicago Divinity School, said, "What's interesting is the disparity . . . [between] the belief that God or the divine controls actions in the world and the reluctance on the part of some to attribute some acts in the world as punishing acts.

"There's a reluctance to think of God as a punishing god. One must look for other explanations for evil in general if one is reluctant to attribute natural disasters to the divine," Coyne said.

"Just by virtue of calling it a 'natural disaster' we're asking is this . . . outside of the reach of the divine?" Coyne said. "Five hundred to 600 years ago, there wouldn't be the assumption necessarily . . . [that] something like this was not directed by divine will."

Regardless of the cause of natural disasters, the survey found that an overwhelming number of respondents—83%—said it was very important or somewhat important to give financial assistance to Japan despite economic troubles in the United States.

Periodical and Internet Sources
Bibliography

The following articles have been chosen to supplement the diverse views presented in this chapter.

Seth Borenstein	"Global Warming Linked to Deadly, Costly Weather Disasters," *USA Today*, March 28, 2012.
Devin Dwyer	"Divine Retribution? Japan Quake, Tsunami Resurface God Debate," ABC News, March 18, 2011. http://abcnews.go.com.
Laura Geller	"Acts of God? A Jewish Perspective on Natural Disasters," *Huffington Post*, April 2, 2011. www.huffingtonpost.com.
Brad Hirschfield	"Does God Cause Natural Disasters?," *Huffington Post*, December 8, 2010. www.huffingtonpost.com.
Wes Isley	"Natural Disasters: God's Anger, the End Times, or Just Reality?," *Huffington Post*, March 28, 2011. www.huffingtonpost.com.
Marc Latham	"Why Does God Test Lifeless Planets with Giant Natural Disasters?," *Suite101*, February 16, 2011. www.suite101.com.
Robert McVie	"Climate Change: Melting Ice Will Trigger Wave of Natural Disasters," *Observer* (London), September 5, 2009.
Solana Pyne	"Extreme Weather: The Reality of a Warming World," *GlobalPost*, January 22, 2011. www.globalpost.com.
Omar Sacirby	"Is God's Wrath at Work in Natural Disasters?," *Washington Post*, May 1, 2010.
Joni Seager	"Eye of the Storm," *Daily Beast*, November 4, 2011. www.thedailybeast.com.

OPPOSING
VIEWPOINTS®
SERIES

CHAPTER 2

What Controversies Surround Disaster Relief Efforts?

Chapter Preface

The devastating earthquake that occurred in Haiti in 2010 had profound political, economic, and social effects. The chaos that reigned in the weeks after the earthquake led to widespread human rights abuses and a rise in human trafficking. In Haiti, 45 percent of the population is under fifteen years of age. Before the earthquake, more than three hundred thousand children and teenagers were already being trafficked inside the country every year. In the earthquake's aftermath, the number was bound to increase. International aid organizations worried that the large number of displaced children would be easy prey for unscrupulous traffickers who could kidnap young children and take them out of the country in the confusion.

Human trafficking has a long and sordid history. The practice can be traced back to ancient times, when young men and women were kidnapped and enslaved by warring groups or tribes and used for labor or forced into sexual slavery. Human trafficking has existed in many societies in different eras.

In the twenty-first century, human trafficking continues to flourish despite international efforts to end it. Natural disasters provide ample opportunity for traffickers to move in and take advantage of the poor and vulnerable. When a devastating tsunami hit Indonesia in 2004, trafficking gangs blanketed the country, kidnapping children and selling them as prostitutes in nearby Malaysia and Jakarta. After the 2005 earthquake in Pakistan, there were reports of traffickers disguising themselves as relatives of hospitalized children and attempting to take them right from their hospital beds. A severe drought in Swaziland in 2007 reportedly led to children being pulled out of school and sold for forced labor or sex. In 2008 a terrible flood occurred in the Indian state of Bihar, and many orphaned and displaced children ended up in relief camps. There they were reportedly lured by human traffickers who promised them jobs and protection but then sold them to brothels across the nation.

Amanda Kloer from Change.org explains the link between natural disasters and human trafficking:

> So how do natural disasters and conflicts turn children into slaves? For the most part, these children were already vulnerable to human trafficking before the disaster struck. They were living at some level of poverty with little education and few resources. The disaster pushes children and their families over the edge into destitution and desperation. Sometimes the disaster causes a family to send a child away to work, a risk that ends in slavery. Sometimes the family must marry off daughters they cannot feed. Sometimes criminal businessmen will traffic children to regain profits lost to a natural disaster. The possibilities are as endless as the supply of children whose lives the disaster has destroyed.

The scourge of human trafficking and other forms of exploitation is one of the issues touched on in the following chapter, which examines some controversies that surround disaster relief efforts. Other viewpoints in the chapter discuss the delivery of relief aid, the role and practices of aid organizations and corporations, and the responsibility of national advocacy organizations to protect the vulnerable in the aftermath of a natural disaster.

> "This repeated scramble for donor
> dollars is just not working."

Aid Organizations Should Not Compete for Assistance Dollars

Saundra Schimmelpfennig

In the following viewpoint, the author states that the way chari-ties raise money in response to natural disaster does not work. She identifies the major problem as a competition for aid dollars, re-sulting in the organizations with the biggest name recognition or celebrity endorser getting the most contributions. Local organiza-tions get overlooked, she asserts, even though they are closer to the ground and better plugged into what communities and individuals need at any given time. She recommends a centralized system for raising and distributing money to ensure that funds get to where they are needed most. Saundra Schimmelpfennig is a blogger and expert on international aid and development.

As you read, consider the following questions:

1. According to Schimmelpfennig, how many aid organiza-tions are responding to the humanitarian crisis in Haiti?

2. According to the UN Office for the Coordination of Humanitarian Affairs, how many nonprofits have offered their assistance following the 2011 Japanese earthquake and tsunami?
3. On what two collaborative efforts would the author like a centralized system for raising and distributing aid money modeled after?

Each high-profile disaster of the past few years—including the Haiti earthquake, Hurricane Katrina, and now the Japan catastrophe [tsunami and nuclear reactor meltdown]—have made it clear that the way charities raise money in response to disasters does not work.

Inevitably, after each disaster a reporter will ask me if enough money or perhaps too much money has been donated. My answer is always the same—some organizations will have too much money and other organizations will have too little money. Often it's not the amount but the distribution that's the problem.

How the System Works

Here's how it works: Charitable donations are the greatest in the first few weeks after a disaster, while it's still making news headlines.

Nonprofits know this, and many of them immediately issue appeals and create advertisements for their disaster response. But this is all done before anybody knows the extent of the disaster, the capacity of the local government and nonprofits to respond, and which other nonprofits are responding and what their capabilities are.

In other words, they raise money in a vacuum.

With each passing disaster, more and more organizations raise money. This leads to intense competition between organizations for donations. Those with the biggest name recognition and the most eye-catching advertising, or those that are on the most lists of "How you can help" or that have the best celebrity endorsers, get the most donations.

The local organizations that are in the midst of the recovery efforts and are working 24 hours a day nonstop have a much harder time raising funds. Many of these groups also have Web sites that are in foreign languages, or they are unable to accept credit-card payments.

In turn, too much money is being raised to support groups that provide things like boats or orphanages, while too little money is raised for help with legal issues or assistance to the elderly. There may be too much money raised by organizations that are incompetent and too little money raised by competent ones.

Coordinating Aid Is Difficult

In the Haiti recovery efforts, somewhere between 1,000 and 10,000 organizations are responding—no one knows the actual number. This makes coordination extremely difficult, increases the chances for gaps and duplication of aid, and makes it impossible to monitor the work of each organization to ensure that programs are done well and don't do any harm.

The March 23 situation report for Japan from the U.N. Office for the Coordination of Humanitarian Affairs says that 670 nonprofits have offered their assistance to provide help following the recent earthquake and tsunami.

This probably means that all 670 of those groups have already raised money for the recovery efforts. And many of them have done this without a clear request for assistance or without identifying local groups to support.

The most recent situation report makes it very clear that Japan is going to allow only very limited international assistance.

So what are all the international charities that raised millions of dollars going to do with all of the money? Here's a statement from Oxfam Japan:

> The Japanese state has the means to reach 99 percent of the population, but there will always be some who need more specific assistance.

And here's a quote from the president of InterAction, a Washington coalition of organizations that work overseas:

> When Hurricane Katrina struck America in 2005, many of the victims of that disaster were comforted from the emotional and monetary support that came from abroad. Just as in Hurricane Katrina, there will sadly be thousands of people who will likely fall through the cracks of Japan's social security net. Japanese civil society, with funds from U.S. and other donors, will help fill that gap. That is where the generosity of the American people and many other nations, make a difference.

So it sounds like the 670 nonprofits that have raised millions of dollars in donations for the recovery efforts will have one of three choices.

If they are allowed, they can compete to provide assistance to the 1 percent of the victims who fall through the cracks. They can try to find local organizations to support, which may mean extra layers of unnecessary bureaucracy and extra work for the local organization to please the group providing the money. Or the organizations may decide to use the money on other disasters or to cover general organizational costs. Some of these groups will be very upfront about this, and some of them will hide it in the fine print.

The system is not working. It's far too opportunistic and does not ensure that money arrives where it is needed the most.

A Possible Solution

Personally, I'd like a centralized system for raising and distributing money. A general fund would be created that people could give to immediately instead of to individual nonprofits. It could operate much like the United Nations Central Emergency Response Fund or the Disasters Emergency Committee appeal, a collaboration of nonprofit groups.

Contributing to a centralized disaster fund would give donors a way to show solidarity with the disaster victims.

Ideally, the money could be distributed by either the government or a coordinating body to ensure that donations go to where they are most needed rather than to whoever can raise the most.

This would potentially help local organizations get the money they need and provide a measure of control over nonprofit work. It would also mean that if all the funds are not needed, they could then be used in disasters that do not get the same media coverage and the same level of financial support.

Some people will argue that the United Nations central fund is too slow or that it favors larger organizations over smaller ones. Both of these are fair criticisms. But then I ask for suggestions on how to create a better system, because this repeated scramble for donor dollars is just not working.

"*People do not lose their basic human rights as a result of a natural disaster [but] . . . are entitled to the protection of all relevant human rights guarantees.*"

National Advocacy Organizations Should Safeguard Disaster Victims' Human Rights

Elizabeth Ferris

In the following viewpoint, a humanitarian assesses the vulnerability of human rights protections after natural disasters, finding that it is the poor and marginalized who are most at risk and suffer disproportionately in times of crisis. These internally displaced persons (IDPs) often face discrimination in aid distribution, enforced relocation, sexual and gender-based violence, and other problems, according to the author. She concedes that although national governments hold the primary responsibility to protect and aid IDPs, the international community should support and supplement these efforts through careful planning, guidance, and consultation with national governments and advocacy groups. Elizabeth Ferris is an author and the codirector of the Brookings-LSE Project on Internal Displacement.

As you read, consider the following questions:
1. What does Ferris believe is the connection between climate change and natural disasters?
2. According to the International Strategy for Disaster Risk Reduction cited by the author, how many people have been affected by natural disasters every year for the past two decades?
3. What does Ferris believe that National Human Rights Institutes should do before a disaster takes place?

A natural disaster is defined by the UN as: "the consequences of events triggered by natural hazards that overwhelm local response capacity and seriously affect the social and economic development of a region." In other words, if an earthquake takes place on an uninhabited island and no one is affected, it is not a natural disaster. In order to be a disaster, people must be affected. Similarly, if flooding takes place in an area where there is adequate preparation, it probably isn't a natural disaster. If a similar level of flooding, however, takes place in an area where there isn't preparation and crops are ruined and people are forced to abandon their homes, it then can be [deemed] a natural disaster. Similarly, heavy rainfalls occur in many parts of the world. Normally, they are not natural disasters, but when the rainfall is heavier than usual and when precautions have not been taken, a natural disaster can result. The rainfall itself is not the disaster, but rather the consequences of the rainfall.

There are two additional aspects of natural disasters that need to be explored before engaging in discussion of human rights and natural disasters.

First, just how "natural" are "natural disasters?" The distinction is often made between natural disasters—such as flooding—

and man-made disasters, such as an oil spill or chemical accident. But often the consequences of natural disasters are worse because of human involvement. To use two examples from my own country: in the 1930s, terrible dust storms in the middle of the United States devastated the lives of inhabitants. For year after year, there was little rainfall, and the topsoil of a major area of the country simply blew away, leaving a swathe of desert. While the lack of rainfall was a natural phenomenon, the fact that a period of intense settlement had converted enormous grasslands into wheat fields and that farmers had plowed up the earth, exposing the soil to the wind was directly responsible for the disaster. If the farmers hadn't settled in the region, if they hadn't plowed up the ground, there would not have been a natural disaster. A second more recent example is Hurricane Katrina, which displaced over a million people in New Orleans and the Gulf coast in 2005. While the hurricane was a natural phenomenon, the fact that the Louisiana wetlands had been destroyed by developers in past decades eliminated a natural barrier for the hurricane. Without the wetlands, the hurricane moved in full force to populated areas, thus causing the disaster. In other words, human actions frequently turn natural weather events into disaster. On this continent [Africa], there are many stories of drought which led to famine and disaster, e.g. Ethiopia in 1984–85, where the famine was a least partly the result of government policies. In fact, [Nobel laureate economist] Amartya Sen has argued that democracies never experience famine because the political pressures force governments to take actions to prevent droughts or other calamities that would otherwise lead to famine.

A second aspect of natural disasters concerns the speed at which they occur. A rapid-onset disaster includes earthquakes, flooding, hurricanes, cyclones, etc. Slow-onset disasters, particularly droughts, develop over a period of time. This gives more time for precautions to be undertaken and for governments and the international community to mitigate the effects of a change in climate. In Southern Africa in 1992 where terrible drought occurred, famine was averted because of policies undertaken by governments in the region and by the international community.

It is generally easier to mobilize international support for sudden-onset disasters; in disasters with high media coverage, there is usually an outpouring of support which is not usually manifest for slow-onset disasters. The outpouring of support for the victims of the 2004 tsunamis, for example, dwarfed the response to victims of flooding in Bangladesh earlier in the year.

Climate Change and Natural Disasters

There has been a lot of speculation about the potential impact of climate change on displacement and some of the speculation is not based on hard evidence. What seems fairly clear, however, is that climate change is likely to increase both the frequency and the severity of natural disasters. It is also likely that global warming will result in sea level rises which may displace people living in low-lying coastal areas or on small islands. There are also predictions that climate change will produce changes in weather patterns which will increase slow-onset disasters, particularly droughts in some regions, including Africa.

Human Rights and Natural Disasters

The International Strategy for Disaster Risk Reduction estimates that 200 million people have been affected by natural disasters every year for the past two decades. In the course of the past year [2008], over 400 natural disasters took 16,000 lives, affected close to 250 million people and displaced many millions.

Most people who are displaced by natural disasters remain within the borders of their country. They are internally displaced persons (IDPs) as defined in the *Guiding Principles on Internal Displacement* and thus entitled to the full range of rights and responsibilities included therein. As with people displaced by conflict, it is their national governments who are responsible for protecting and assisting them and with facilitating durable solutions for their displacement.

The Role of Poverty

We know that poverty and marginalization makes things worse for victims of natural disasters. Natural disasters in poorer countries have higher casualties than disasters of similar magnitude in wealthier countries. Within countries, it is often the marginalized groups who suffer disproportionately. In Colombia and the Philippines, for example, it is usually poorer, marginalized groups who live on the slopes of volcanoes. People with more resources choose to live elsewhere. And so, when the volcanoes erupt, it is the poor who suffer disproportionately. In Central America and Brazil, it is the poor who live in shantytowns on the hills surrounding major cities—hills which are susceptible to mudslides at times of heavy rain. We know that women are more likely to die in floods by a factor of 3 or 4 to 1 than men. Children, the elderly, the disabled and the sick are also more likely to suffer as a result of natural disasters.

Operational Guidelines

In the aftermath of the 2004 tsunami, there was recognition that disaster response involves more than delivery of humanitarian assistance. Growing recognition of the need to respect, uphold, and promote the human rights of those affected by natural disasters, whether displaced or not, was the driving force between efforts by the RSG [Representative of the UN Secretary-General on the Human Rights of Internally Displaced Persons] to develop Operational Guidelines for Human Rights and Natural Disasters. These guidelines, which were formally adopted by the InterAgency Standing Committee in June 2006, are presently being used to train disaster responders on ways of ensuring that human rights are protected in the midst of disaster.

The problems that are often encountered by persons affected by the consequences of natural disasters include: unequal access to assistance; discrimination in aid provision; enforced reloca-tion; sexual and gender-based violence; loss of documentation; recruitment of children into fighting forces; unsafe or involun-tary return or resettlement; and issues of property restitution.

The Guidelines suggest a human rights approach to planning both the initial emergency and longer-term response. People do not lose their basic human rights as a result of a natural disaster or their displacement. Rather all of those affected by natural di-sasters, including those who are displaced, are entitled to the pro-tection of all relevant human rights guarantees. As residents, and usually citizens of the country in which they are living, they are entitled to the protections afforded to all residents and citizens even though they may have particular needs related to the disas-ter and thus require specific assistance and protection measures.

As with all situations of internal displacement, the primary duty and responsibility to provide such protection and assistance lies with the national authorities of the affected countries. Those affected by natural disasters have the right to request and receive such protection and assistance from their governments.

Four Groups of Human Rights

The Operational Guidelines stress that human rights encom-pass not only civil and political rights but also economic, social and cultural rights. However, in the midst of a disaster, it is of-ten difficult to simultaneously promote all rights for all of those affected. Thus for practical reasons, the Operational Guidelines divide human rights into four groups, namely:

A. rights related to physical security and integrity (e.g. protection of the right to life and the right to be free of as-sault, rape, arbitrary detention, kidnapping, and threats to these rights);

B. rights related to basic necessities of life (e.g. the rights to food, drinking water, shelter, adequate clothing, adequate health services, and sanitation);

C. rights related to other economic, social and cultural protection needs (e.g. the rights to be provided with or have
access to education, to receive restitution or compensation
for lost property, and to work); and

D. rights related to other civil and political protection needs
(e.g. the rights to religious freedom and freedom of
speech, personal documentation, political participation,
access to courts, and freedom from discrimination).

The Operational Guidelines suggest that the first two groups
of rights may be the most relevant during the emergency, life-
saving phase. Thus in the initial disaster response, it is usually
more important to ensure adequate access to water than to provide replacement identity cards to those who have been displaced. However, the guidelines insist that only the full respect
of all four groups of rights can ensure adequate protection of the
human rights of those affected by natural disasters, including of
those who are displaced.

The guidelines go on to state that "in all cases States have an
obligation to respect, protect and to fulfill the human rights of
their citizens and of any other persons in their territory or under
their jurisdiction." States thus have a responsibility: to prevent
violations of these rights from occurring or re-occurring; to stop
them when they do occur, and to ensure reparation and full rehabilitation if a violation has happened.

The International Community's Role

When governments are unwilling or unable to fulfill these responsibilities, the international community needs to support and
supplement the efforts of the government and local authorities.
And these organizations as well—UN agencies, international
and national non-governmental organizations, civil society, and
IDP communities themselves—have a responsibility to ensure
that their approaches and programs incorporate a human rights
focus.

In fact, most often, rights are violated not because of conscious intention but because of the lack of awareness or planning based on a rights-based approach. Thus in the United States, the evacuation plans for New Orleans in 2005 were based on private vehicles—even though there were racial and class differences in vehicle ownership. While most middle class white people had access to private cars, many poor and African-American residents did not. More recently, in the evacuation of New Orleans prior to Hurricane Gustav in August 2008, it was clear that officials had still not heeded the lessons learned from Katrina. While evacuation plans provided bus transportation for those without cars, displaced New Orleans residents were taken by bus to large communal shelters while those who evacuated by car were directed to churches, private homes and hotels.

Experience has shown while patterns of discrimination emerge during the initial emergency response phase, the longer that displacement lasts, the greater the risk of human rights violations.

The Brookings-Bern Project on Internal Displacement developed a manual on the Operational Guidelines to provide more concrete guidance to disaster responders, and this manual is currently being revised in light of experiences in the field. Presently both Brookings and the Protection Cluster Working Group are organizing training sessions for government officials responsible for disaster response as well as non-governmental organizations. Such training is necessary in order to ensure that a rights-based approach to disaster response is incorporated into all phases of operations.

The Role of National Human Rights Institutions

National Human Rights Institutions [NHRIs] are well-placed to play a role in upholding human rights standards for those affected by natural disasters. Last year [2007], some of you participated in a session led by Joyce Leader who was working with us,

Guiding Principles on Internal Displacement

In 1998, I introduced *Guiding Principles on Internal Displacement* into the United Nations to draw international attention to the needs of internally displaced persons and to enhance protection for them. Developed by a team of international legal experts, in collaboration with international agencies and nongovernmental organizations, the thirty principles set forth the rights of internally displaced persons and the obligations of governments, nonstate actors and international organizations toward these populations.

Although the *Guiding Principles* themselves are not a binding legal document comparable to a treaty, they are based on and consistent with international human rights law, humanitarian law, and refugee law by analogy. Their acknowledgment in resolutions of the UN Commission on Human Rights and Economic and Social Council [ECOSOC] underscores the moral authority they have begun to command. In his report to ECOSOC in 1998, the Secretary-General listed them as one of the notable achievements in the humanitarian area for that year.

Frances M. Deng, foreword to the
Handbook for Applying the Guiding
Principles on Internal Displacement, *The*
Brookings Institution, 1999.

to explore some of the ways that NHRIs can become involved in monitoring displacement. I'd like to share with you some of the experiences of NHRIs in another part of the world—Asia—to see if their experiences could be helpful to you in Africa. At its meeting in September 2001, the Asia Pacific Forum of National

Human Rights Institutions expressed interest in developing their capacity to promote and respect the human rights of IDPs. In March 2005, following the December 2004 tsunamis, the NHRIs met again and agreed on the need to develop a common methodology for their role with regard to IDPs in the context of natural disasters. In August 2005, the members of the Asia Pacific Forum welcomed draft guidelines which were not introduced as binding instruments, but rather as good practices which might be useful to NHRIs experiencing natural disasters.

I'd like to share some of these guidelines with you.

The Guidelines

Strengthening NHRI capacity. There are many strategies to strengthen NHRIs' capacities. Immediate strategies consist of appointing an IDP focal point, establishing links with regional areas, training and providing relevant documents about human rights issues faced by IDPs to staff member and integrating local legal and IDP experts. During an emergency response to a natural disaster, NHRIs should develop a comprehensive approach to the promotion and protection of human rights and establish short team offices in the affected areas. After the immediate effects of the disaster subside, NHRIs should establish a strategy to address IDP concerns with all relevant sections of the NHRI.

Working with government. In order for NHRIs to work effectively with the government during a disaster, before a disaster takes place NHRIs should disseminate the Guiding Principles to government agencies, advocate for the ratification of all relevant international human rights and humanitarian instruments and identify gaps in the laws and recommend reforms. While there is an emergency response, organize a public hearing, ensure the government has a rights-based approach to the provision of aid, and work with the government to ensure they reissue identity papers and other documents. In the long term, NHRIs must encourage the government to develop an effective rights-based policy, meet with government agencies engaged in work with IDPs to gather accurate information, and recommend that the government establish a formal taskforce to share information.

Working with UN, civil society and other non-state actors. Communication with the UN, civil society and other non-state actors should begin before a natural disaster takes place. While working with these groups it is essential to disseminate the Guiding Principles, advise on the risks to the human rights of IDPs and seek advice from the UN and other relevant actors. During an emergency response, NHRIs must ensure the participation of IDPs in all processes and engage both state and non-state actors about the risks face by IDPs. After a disaster NHRIs must monitor the state of IDPs, contribute to UN monitoring mechanisms and help with rehabilitation, compensation and reconstruction for IDPs.

Awareness-raising. To increase awareness among local populations the Guiding Principles should be translated into all relevant languages and dialects and distributed. During a natural disaster it is imperative to develop a public information strategy to raise awareness for human rights issues for IDPs, as well as go to the affected areas to meet with IDPs, international and national NGOs and the government to determine the effects of the disaster. There are many different long term projects that NHRIs can take part in to increase awareness including, providing and disseminating on-going coverage of human rights issues caused by natural disasters, integrating the human rights implications of internal displacement into training, participating in international conferences, workshops, and seminars, and stressing the need for a rights-based approach to humanitarian assistance.

Complaint handling. In order to effectively handle complaints during a natural disaster, NHRIs must establish relationships with all complaint hearing mechanisms in various communities and ensure that these complaint hearing mechanisms have the flexibility to function throughout an emergency. In an emergency response it is important for NHRIs to publicize complaint handling functions to the IDP population and help seek out complaints from the IDP population. In the long term, NHRIs should take part in court proceedings and advocate for the prosecution of individuals that violate human rights.

Regional Cooperation. Internal displacement is not only an issue internal to a country but the entire region. Cooperation between NHRIs should be multilateral through information sharing and the organization of seminars and workshops.

For discussion:
- To what extent do these guidelines, developed in Asia, make sense for Africa?
- What do you see as the main barriers to your more effective engagement with IDPs and with Natural Disasters?

National Human Rights Institutions are uniquely placed to play a role in ensuring that the human rights of those affected by natural disasters are promoted. You have the expertise in human rights principles and the mandate to protect human rights. You are rooted in your own local and national context and thus may have a better view of what is needed and what is possible than international actors. While specific national contexts vary and different kinds of disasters require different responses, the need to uphold human rights in emergency situations seems to be a constant. We look forward to hearing from you about the kinds of natural disasters you have lived through and your views on possible actions which you could take to ensure that the human rights of the victims of natural disasters are upheld.

> "[Relief] contracts are awarded as part
> of a corporate agenda that sees disaster
> as an opportunity, a tool for furthering
> policies that would not be possible in
> other times."

Corporations Are Profiting from Disaster Relief Contracts at the Expense of Victims

Jordan Flaherty

In the following viewpoint, a journalist posits that much of the promised relief and reconstruction aid earmarked to rebuild Haiti after the 2010 earthquake did not reach those who need it. In fact, he reports, a closer look at what is happening in the country reveals a corrupt corporate agenda that aims to exploit natural disasters for financial gain. Corporations are enriching themselves at the expense of victims, and the US government is not intervening to stop corporate profiteering, he asserts. He suggests that not only are corporations benefiting but relief and aid groups are also finding ways to take advantage of a massive outpouring of donations meant to help people and rebuild infrastructures. Jordan Flaherty is a reporter, author, and staffer with the Louisiana Justice Institute.

As you read, consider the following questions:
1. Who is Gilbert Bigio, according to Flaherty?
2. According to the Stafford Act as cited by Flaherty, contracting officials must give what percentage of rebuilding contracts to minority-owned businesses?
3. According to a recent report from the Disaster Accountability Project (DAP) cited by the author, what has happened to much of the donations for Haiti?

One year after an earthquake devastated Haiti, much of the promised relief and reconstruction aid has not reached those most in need. In fact, the nation's tragedy has served as an opportunity to further enrich corporate interests.

The details of a recent lawsuit, as reported by *Businessweek*, highlights the ways in which contractors—including some of the same players who profited from Hurricane Katrina–related reconstruction—have continued to use their political connections to gain profits from others' suffering, receiving contracts worth tens of millions of dollars while the Haitian people receive pennies at best. It also demonstrates ways in which charity and development efforts have mirrored and contributed to corporate abuses.

The AshBritt Situation

Lewis Lucke, a 27-year veteran of the US Agency for International Development (US AID) was named US special coordinator for relief and reconstruction after the earthquake. He worked this job for a few months, then immediately moved to the private sector, where he could sell his contacts and connections to the highest bidder. He quickly got a $30,000-a-month (plus bonuses) contract with the Haiti Recovery Group (HRG).

HRG had been founded by AshBritt, Inc., a Florida-based contractor who had received acres of bad press for their post-Katrina contracting. AshBritt's partner in HRG is Gilbert Bigio, a wealthy Haitian businessman with close ties to the Israeli military. Bigio made a fortune during the corrupt [Jean-Claude] Duvalier regime and was a supporter of the right-wing coup against Haitian president [Jean-Bertrand] Aristide.

Although Lucke received $60,000 for two months' work, he is suing because he says he is owed an additional $500,000 for the more than $20 million in contracts he helped HRG obtain during that time.

As CorpWatch has reported, AshBritt "has enjoyed meteoric growth since it won its first big debris removal subcontract from none other than Halliburton [an American corporation long associated with both Bush administrations], to help clean up after Hurricane Andrew in 1992." In 1999, the company also faced allegations of double billing for $765,000 from the Broward County, Florida school board for clean-up done in the aftermath of Hurricane Wilma.

AshBritt CEO Randal Perkins is a major donor to Republican causes and hired Mississippi Governor Haley Barbour's firm, as well as former US Army Corps of Engineers official Mike Parker, as lobbyists. As a reward for his political connections, AshBritt won $900 million in post-Katrina contracts, helping them to become the poster child for political corruption in the world of disaster profiteering, even triggering a congressional investigation focusing on their buying of influence. MSNBC reported in early 2006 that criticism of AshBritt "can be heard in virtually every coastal community between Alabama and Texas."

Privatizing Disaster Relief

The contracts given to Bush cronies like AshBritt resulted in local and minority-owned companies losing out on reconstruction work. As *Multinational Monitor* noted shortly after Katrina, "by turning the contracting process over to prime contractors like AshBritt, the [Army] Corps [of Engineers] and FEMA [Federal Emergency Management Agency] have effectively privatized the enforcement of Federal Acquisition Regulations and disaster relief laws such as the Stafford Act, which require contracting officials to prioritize local businesses and give 5 percent of contracts to minority-owned businesses. As a result ... early reports suggest that over 90 percent of the $2 billion in initial contracts was awarded to companies based outside of the three primary affected states, and that minority businesses received just 1.5 percent of the first $1.6 billion."

Alex Dupuy, writing in the *Washington Post,* reported a similar pattern in Haiti, noting that "of the more than 1,500 US contracts doled out worth $267 million, only 20, worth $4.3 million, have gone to Haitian firms. The rest have gone to US firms, which almost exclusively use US suppliers. Although these foreign contractors employ Haitians, mostly on a cash-for-work basis, the bulk of the money and profits are reinvested in the United States." The same article notes that "less than 10 percent of the $9 billion pledged by foreign donors has been delivered, and not all of that money has been spent. Other than rebuilding the international airport and clearing the principal urban arteries of rubble, no major infrastructure rebuilding—roads, ports, housing, communications—has begun."

Disaster Profiteering

The disaster profiteering exemplified by AshBritt is not just the result of quick decision-making in the midst of a crisis. These contracts are awarded as part of a corporate agenda that sees disaster as an opportunity, a tool for furthering policies that would not be possible in other times. [Canadian critic of corporations] Naomi Klein exposed evidence that, within 24 hours of the earthquake, the influential right-wing think tank the Heritage Foundation was already laying plans to use the disaster as an attempt at further privatization of the country's economy.

Relief and recovery efforts, led by the US military, have also brought a further militarization of relief and criminalization of survivors. Haiti and Katrina also served as staging grounds for increased involvement of mercenaries in reconstruction efforts.

The Earthquake in Haiti

- On January 12 [2010] at 1653 hours [4:53 PM] local time, a magnitude 7.0 earthquake struck southern Haiti. According to the U.S. Geological Survey (USGS), the earthquake's epicenter was located 10 miles southwest of the capital Port-au-Prince, West Department. The earthquake killed an estimated 230,000 people and affected approximately 3 million others, according to the GoH [government of Haiti]. On January 13, U.S. Ambassador to Haiti Kenneth H. Merten declared a disaster due to the effects of the earthquake.

- During the months following the earthquake, humanitarian efforts met the immediate needs of earthquake-affected populations, through the provision of safe drinking water, food, household items, shelter assistance, and health care. USAID continues to work closely with other U.S. Government agencies, the GoH, international organizations, the U.N., and NGOs [nongovernmental organizations] to coordinate ongoing efforts and to facilitate the transition from emergency relief activities to recovery operations, while preparing to respond to the potential for further deterioration in humanitarian conditions during the rainy and hurricane seasons.

"Haiti—Earthquake," USAID,
September 3, 2010.

As one Blackwater mercenary told [investigative journalist] Jeremy Scahill when he visited New Orleans in the days after Katrina, "This is a trend. You're going to see a lot more guys like us in these situations."

And it's not just corporations who have been guilty of profiting from Haitian suffering. A recent report from the Disaster Accountability Project (DAP) describes a "significant lack of transparency in the disaster-relief/aid community," and finds that many relief organizations have left donations for Haiti in their bank accounts, earning interest rather than helping the people of Haiti. DAP director Ben Smilowitz notes that "the fact that nearly half of the donated dollars still sit in the bank accounts of relief and aid groups does not match the urgency of their own fundraising and marketing efforts and donors' intentions, nor does it covey the urgency of the situation on the ground."

Haitian poet and human rights lawyer Ezili Dantò has written,

> Haiti's poverty began with a US/Euro trade embargo after its independence, continued with the Independence Debt to France and ecclesiastical and financial colonialism. Moreover, in more recent times, the uses of US foreign aid, as administered through USAID in Haiti, basically serves to fuel conflicts and covertly promote US corporate interests to the detriment of democracy and Haitian health, liberty, sovereignty, social justice and political freedoms. USAID projects have been at the frontlines of orchestrating undemocratic behavior, bringing underdevelopment, coup d'etat, impunity of the Haitian Oligarchy, indefinite incarceration of dissenters, and destroying Haiti's food sovereignty essentially promoting famine.

Since before the earthquake, Haiti has been a victim of many of those who have claimed they are there to help. Until we address this fundamental issue of corporate profiteering masquerading as aid and development, the nation will remain mired in poverty. And future disasters, wherever they occur, will lead to similar injustices.

> *"Aid . . . ultimately led to more
> division, more cynicism and made
> the mercantile class even richer."*

Relief Efforts Contribute to Increased Corruption and Poverty Following Natural Disasters

Ian Birrell

*In the following viewpoint, the author outlines the deficiencies of
the global relief industry as revealed in the horrible situation in
Haiti. As the international community donated billions of dollars
to help victims and rebuild the country after the 2010 earthquake,
he reports, the situation got worse instead of better: prices for basic
necessities skyrocketed, sanitation and security deteriorated, corruption was rampant, and people were forced from damaged homes
into squalid and dangerous refugee camps. Many of the promises
made by relief organizations have been broken, he maintains, and
victims have been left with little. No matter how well-intentioned
relief efforts are, he concludes, they have done little for the people
who need the most aid. Ian Birrell is a reporter for the* Daily Mail,
a London newspaper.

Ian Birrell, "Haiti and the Shaming of the Aid Zealots: How Donated Billions Have
INCREASED Poverty and Corruption," *Daily Mail*, January 27, 2012. Reproduced by
permission.

As you read, consider the following questions:
1. How much money has the international community contributed to rebuild Haiti, according to the author?
2. How many Haitians does Birrell say remain in squalid refugee camps?
3. According to Birrell, what was Haiti's nickname?

The first thing that strikes you is the smell: a sweet, sickly stench that sticks to your skin. It is worst in the morning, since women are terrified of risking a nocturnal trip to the handful of lavatories serving the thousands of people in the camp because of an epidemic of rape. Even the youngest girls are in danger.

The Situation Has Not Changed

I stop to chat to a young man in a green polo shirt. Ricardo Jenty says we must take care because three gunmen have just walked by on their way to settle a feud. He fears trouble; already he has seen friends shot dead.

Ricardo, 25, a father of three young children, recounts how the earthquake that hit Haiti two years ago [2010] ruined his home and wrecked his life. His makeshift tent is one of thousands crammed onto what was once a football pitch [field].

"Every day there are fights between gangs. There are so many young bloods that don't care now. You have to avoid them—most of us don't want any part of these things."

Ricardo lifts the faded sheet that serves as his front door. His three-week-old baby lies asleep on the single bed that fills the family's home, while his two-year old son screams at the back entrance.

The heat under the plastic roof is so intense his wife Roseline, 27, drips with sweat as she describes living in such hell. She looks exhausted. If she is lucky, she says, she has one meal a day, but often goes two days without food, putting salt in water to keep her going.

Since giving birth she has passed out a number of times and does not produce enough breast milk to feed her new son. She shows me a small can of condensed milk she gives him; she cannot afford the baby formula he needs.

So had they seen any of the huge sums of aid donated to alleviate such hardship? They shake their heads—just one hygiene kit from the local Red Cross. "I have heard about this aid but never seen it," says Roseline. "I don't think people like us stood a chance of getting any of it."

Ricardo says it makes him angry. "If I looked back two years ago I would never have thought I would still be here in this camp. If the aid organisations really cared about our lives, they could have done something. But how can I have hope for my future, living like this?"

An International Shame

The family's story shames all those international organisations that flocked to Haiti after the earthquake two years ago, which killed an estimated 225,000 people. It was one of the most devastating natural disasters of recent years—and the world responded in sympathy. The international community claimed to have given £6.5 billion to heal Haiti's wounds, while donations poured in to charities.

Earlier this month [January 2012], on the quake's second anniversary, aid agencies pumped out press releases proclaiming their successes. Add up all the people they claim to have helped and the number exceeds the population of Haiti.

The reality is rather different—and shines a stark light on the assumptions, arrogance and deficiencies of the ever-growing global relief industry. As promises were broken, mistakes were made and money was wasted, prices of food and basic supplies for local people soared, sanitation deteriorated, there was less safe water to drink and well-meaning interventions made matters infinitely worse.

United Nations peacekeepers, supposedly there to protect local people, presided over the world's deadliest cholera outbreak that has killed nearly 7,000 people and infected half a million more.

Only 4,769 new houses have been built, and 13,578 homes repaired, while 520,000 people remain in those squalid camps. Many more returned to wrecked homes rather than endure the camps' inhuman conditions, blamed for driving up violence, rape and paedophilia.

A Bad Situation Gets Worse

"Aid did some good and saved some lives early on but ultimately led to more division, more cynicism and made the mercantile class even richer," says Mark Schuller, a U.S. anthropologist who teaches in Haiti. "In the end the way the aid was delivered, the lack of co-ordination and the lack of respect for the Haitian people did more harm than good. It would have been better if they had not come."

Schuller, who spends $375 per month renting his three-bedroom flat, is critical of humanitarian staff earning up to ten times local salaries, with big cars, drivers and $2,500-a-month housing allowances. Rents have soared since the quake.

Haiti's prime minister has pointed out that 40 percent of aid money supports the foreigners handing it out. Undoubtedly, huge sums have been wasted: for example, humanitarian groups paid double local rates for lorry [truck] loads of water.

One car dealer sold more than 250 Toyota Land Cruisers a month at £40,000 each. "You see traffic jams at Friday lunchtime of all the white NGO [nongovernmental organizations] and UN four-wheel drives heading off early to the beaches for the weekend," said one Irish aid worker. "It makes me sick."

Haiti's History

Haiti had huge problems even before the earthquake ripped it apart in 35 terrifying seconds. The poorest nation in the western hemisphere, it has had a turbulent history since a slave revolt against French colonial masters led to independence in 1804.

It suffered from suffocating foreign interference and a succession of brutal, hopeless and hapless governments. In the past

25 years alone Haiti has endured nine presidents, two coups and one invasion.

It has also received astounding amounts of aid: in the half century before the quake, Haiti was handed four times as much per capita as Europeans received under the post-[World War II] Marshall plan. There were more charities in Haiti—an estimated 12,000—on the ground per head of population than any other place on earth.

Over the same period incomes collapsed by more than one-third in a nation nicknamed "The Republic of NGOs." It is hard not to wonder if the torrents of aid were one cause of the nation's problems, creating a culture of dependency, fostering corruption and undermining its image.

After the quake, the world rushed to help again. But many official pledges of assistance turned out to be little more than lies, with half the promised funds never turning up and huge slices of the rest diverted back to donors. The largest single recipient of U.S. earthquake aid, for example, was the U.S. government.

Meanwhile, Haitians themselves were largely ignored. A study of nearly 1,500 contracts awarded by U.S. authorities found only 23 went to Haitian companies while contractors based in Washington received more than one-third of funds—hardly the best way to help Haiti's development.

How the Aid Got Spent

As images of biblical devastation played out on the news, aid-groups were flooded with donations, but substantial sums remain unspent. Major charities still hold one-third of the cash they raised; the American Red Cross alone has more cash in its coffers than the £107 million donated to the disaster by Britons.

Devastated areas were plastered with logos and flags as charities fought to get in front of the cameras and tap into the goldrush. One U.S. preacher held up traffic on a main road as he filmed a video of himself handing a bag of rice to a kneeling

Haitian; another flew in by private jet from Texas to make fund-raising videos using orphans as props.

One aid group stood apart: Médecins Sans Frontières [Doctors Without Borders]—which had worked in Haiti for 20 years—closed its appeal after a few days as it had raised enough for immediate needs.

Gaetan Drossart, its head of mission, said it was wrong for charities to raise more than they could spend. "Organisations want to be in front of the cameras in an emergency to attract attention since this gets the money," he said. "The humanitarian business is no different to any other business." Drossart wants limits placed on the numbers of groups allowed in to disaster zones given the chaos and poor co-ordination he witnessed in the earthquake's aftermath.

A Dangerous Situation

Just down the road from his office colourful wooden sheds called Transitional Shelters dot the landscape. These tiny temporary homes were built not because survivors wanted them—they would have preferred to have ruined properties rebuilt or new homes—but because donors wanted visible signs of progress.

They are taking twice as long and—at £345 million—nearly three times as much money to build as planned. The flagship community was Corail, about ten miles outside Port-au-Prince. Families were lured here with promises of clean water, medical care, education and jobs in proposed garment factories. The actor Sean Penn, who spent several months in Haiti after the quake, was among those who persuaded people to move.

Now these unfortunate people are marooned on a rocky patch of land: the factories have not materialised, there are no hospitals, the schools are inadequate and they have started being charged for water at more than twice the cost in the camps. Vast squatter camps have sprung up on the hillsides around them.

"They promised us when we came here we would find everything we needed," said Marjorie Saint Hilaire, a mother of three

"Disaster relief—the experts arrive," cartoon by Paul Fitzgerald. www.CartoonStock.com.

boys whose husband was killed in the quake. "Now we are living in a desert."

Pregnant women have died trying to get to hospital, a journey that can take three hours on four different buses. Two days before my visit, a woman in labour had to take a motorcycle to hospital.

Fernande Bien Amie, a mother of two, said they felt betrayed by aid groups reneging on promises and by their government's failure to monitor them. "These NGOs just do whatever they want, then leave whenever they want," she said.

Good Intentions Gone Wrong

As so often with the aid industry, for all its undoubted achievements in difficult conditions, good intentions keep backfiring. Camps were given soap but no water, condoms but not food. Text messages told people to wash before eating when babies were being bathed in sewer water.

Payments for rubble clearance led people to stop clearing streets until given money.

Curiously, it was in the notorious ghetto of Cité Soleil—avoided as too dangerous by many relief groups—that I found the most hopeful signs of Haiti's rebirth. Young activists are cleaning up the streets, going out with brushes to sweep away rubbish, unblock evil-smelling canals and foster communal pride. The results are impressive.

"People come to our meetings as they want to see our streets clean," says Robillard Lovino, 25, one of the organisers. "It's not a foreign NGO telling them to do things, this is communities figuring out their own change."

In a decrepit building, students are crammed into classes in journalism, theatre, dance and music organised by Hilaire Jean Lesly, director of a community radio station. "We have no help and have not asked for help—Haitians must take responsibility for themselves," he says.

"We want to show the good side of Cité Soleil. You only hear bad things about gangsters, violence and poverty," said Lesly. "NGOs just want to show places like this as weak and vulnerable because that justifies always asking for their help."

Harsh words. But as the aid industry moves off in search of new emergencies and new funds, perhaps it should listen to such voices.

> "There is evidence that disasters can
> be agents of progress—especially in
> wealthier countries."

Only Wealthy Countries Can Recover from Natural Disasters

John Mutter

In the following viewpoint, a researcher contends that natural disasters are catastrophic for small countries or regions, but not for larger and wealthier countries. In fact, he argues, natural disasters may provide economic progress for wealthy countries because they force widespread upgrades to infrastructure essential to commerce. Furthermore, he asserts, wealthy countries have the economic resources to absorb the damage in the long term. A poor country like Haiti can be plunged into economic free fall by a devastating natural disaster, while a rich country like Japan can actually show improvement after one, he concludes. John Mutter is a professor in the Department of Earth and Environmental Sciences at Columbia University in New York City.

As you read, consider the following questions:
1. What did G7 nations do immediately after the 2011 earthquake in Japan, according to Mutter?
2. Where does the author say that most of the wealth is produced in Japan?
3. According to Mutter, what are the four components of GDP?

In the hours (not days) after the enormous earthquake hit Japan on March 11 [2011], before it was even known that the Fukushima power plant had been badly disabled and well before the scope of the mortality and damage had been assessed, the Japanese yen rapidly appreciated in value. The G7 nations [the top seven wealthiest nations] moved to quickly stabilize the yen—not to prevent it from falling, but to prevent it from further appreciating.

From a geophysical point of view this earthquake and tsunami rank among the very worst things that nature can throw at us. But most economists are saying that this disaster will not hurt the Japanese economy very much. Large disasters, it turns out, are not bad for the economies of wealthier countries, including Japan. In fact, in strange ways, large disasters can actually provide economic progress.

Earthquakes, hurricanes, floods and other such disasters all cause damage in relatively restricted areas, even if those areas seem fairly large. Unless the disaster makes a direct hit on an industry that is particularly critical to a country's economy, the rest of the country can often buffer the effect.

Size Matters

The U.S., for example, is so large geographically, and its economy is also so large and diversified, that it is hard to imagine a natural disaster that would seriously impact the total national economy for very long. Regional economies, of course, can be seriously affected—but even Hurricane Katrina went relatively unnoticed in the national economy.

It makes sense then that small countries would experience greater impacts. Hurricane Mitch's strike on Honduras in 1998 was so devastating that Honduran President Carlos Roberto Flores said that economic progress in the country had been set back 50 years. That wasn't quite true, but he could hardly be blamed for thinking it might be, given the devastation of that event. Virtually every corner of the country was affected. Other small countries, including Fiji, Samoa, St. Lucia and Madagascar have had similar experiences. Large countries, and wealthier countries, have not.

In Japan, most of the wealth is produced from Tokyo southward. The northern region hit by the tsunami accounts for a very small fraction of the country's gross domestic product (GDP). Fishing and farming are just not big parts of the Japanese economy. The Fukushima nuclear plant is another story, of course, and given that it supplies Tokyo with power, the disaster there is felt well outside the directly affected area. Still, the Japanese economy has not tanked, and most pundits say it isn't going to.

Stabilizing the yen also helped Japan's economy, especially in the short-term. A stronger yen isn't good for the Japanese economy, because it makes Japanese goods more expensive on foreign markets and Japan is a major exporting nation. The immediate spike in the yen came about because currency traders (speculators) thought that yen would become scarce and started buying up the currency and driving up the price. The speculation was that Japanese people have many of their investments outside the country and would want to bring their money back home to help them recover from the disaster. This would mean changing investments made in foreign currency back into yen, which would increase pressure on the yen and raise its price. It was the *speculation* that this would occur that drove up the price; there wasn't any actual run on the yen.

Speculative impulses shouldn't surprise us too much, and unless they get out of control, they shouldn't hurt too much either. Markets usually correct themselves when the perceived reason for speculative buying (or selling) proves to be false.

Agents of Progress

But there is a deeper, and seemingly more perverse, economic current running through many disasters: There is evidence that disasters can be agents of progress—especially in wealthier countries. This is more than the short-term bump you might expect in the building industry.

Think about it in the same way a homeowner can use an insurance claim for fire damage to make needed home improvements. No one would replace kitchen appliances damaged in a fire with the same old models. We would all want to upgrade.

Now translate that to a national scale. If the infrastructure essential to commerce (bridges, roads, port facilities) that was washed away in a hurricane or tsunami were old and inefficient (as is often the case), and if it could be quickly replaced by much better infrastructure—particularly if that can be done using external aid, say, from the World Bank—then a lasting benefit to a country's economy might ensue. Resources contributed to relief efforts are equivalent to an economic stimulus package.

Another Injustice

So should we not worry about disasters? Should we just sit back, let them happen and reap the benefits?

I'm afraid not. Alas, only wealthy nations, or regions, seem to reap any "benefits." Certainly Haiti hasn't seen any economic benefits since the 2010 earthquake, and although much of New Orleans has come back following Hurricane Katrina, the Lower 9th Ward probably hasn't seen much windfall, nor has the coastline of Indonesia that was destroyed in the 2004 tsunami, or any other very poor place, as far as I can tell. Perhaps the potential for a disaster windfall is just another expression of the injustice of disasters. It may even be deeply misleading.

The standard measure of an economy is GDP, the market value of all final goods and services produced within a country. It sums four components: private consumption, gross investments, government spending and the value of exports minus imports.

Usually GDP per capita is employed as a welfare measure, but it is routinely criticized as imperfect, especially as a measure of the state of poor countries where so much of the economy is at subsistence level. Look at the components of GDP and it isn't hard to see why they might all increase after a disaster—but only for countries with a lot of consumers, many investors, good government institutions and significant exports.

Other losses—such as the deaths of people who were not consuming, investing and producing exports—also don't alter the balance of a GDP-measured economy. The economic hit a country takes from a disaster bears little relationship to mortality figures. Even the extremely high mortality events so common in poor countries only remove a small fraction of the total population and an even smaller fraction of the tax-paying workforce. So to the GDP economy, high death tolls are not of interest. No wonder economics is known as the dismal science.

What this all means is that standard economics will generally overlook the harm disasters cause to those in poorer countries and to poorer people everywhere. It is the profound injustice of disasters.

Periodical and Internet Sources Bibliography

The following articles have been chosen to supplement the diverse views presented in this chapter.

Tom Bateman	"Charities Deny 'Scramble' for Japan Aid Cash," *BBC News*, March 30, 2011. www.bbc.co.uk.
Joel Charny	"Traditional Humanitarian Aid Is Vital," *Guardian*, April 13, 2011.
Paul Clolery	"The Preparedness and Resilience Foundation Act: Should Government Compete with Aid Organizations?," *Huffington Post*, April 27, 2012. www.huffington post.com.
Andrea Rees Davies	"Disaster Relief Aid Must Aid Rich and Poor," *San Francisco Chronicle*, April 17, 2012.
Michel Gabaudan	"From Emergency Aid to Development Aid: Agencies Are Failing to Connect," *Guardian*, January 19, 2012.
Carl Hulse	"Federal Austerity Changes Disaster Relief," *New York Times*, August 30, 2011.
Tom Jacobs	"Not All Suffering Prompts Equal Generosity," *Pacific Standard*, January 7, 2011.
Nicholas D. Kristof	"Getting Smart on Aid," *New York Times*, May 18, 2011.
David Luhnow	"Global Aid Is No Relief for Small Haitian Businesses," *Wall Street Journal*, March 3, 2010.
Lydia Polgreen	"The Special Pain of a Slow Disaster," *New York Times*, November 10, 2010.
Donovan Webster	"Haiti: Two Years After the Earthquake, Where Did the Money Go?," *GlobalPost*, January 10, 2012. www.globalpost.com.

CHAPTER 3

What Should Be the Government's Role in Natural Disaster Relief?

Chapter Preface

In the United States, the Federal Emergency Management Agency (FEMA) coordinates the federal government's role in "preparing for, preventing, mitigating the effects of, responding to, and recovering from all domestic disasters, whether natural or man-made, including acts of terror." Throughout the years, the agency has received both praise and criticism for its response to various natural disasters. FEMA has also spurred controversy across the political spectrum because it reflects the enduring American concern with the role of federal government and government programs. FEMA generates debate because its performance makes such a fundamental difference in how America prepares, reacts to, and recovers from a terrorist attack, national emergency, or natural disaster.

The origins of FEMA can be traced back to the Congressional Act of 1803, which is widely considered to be the first piece of disaster legislation in the United States. The act offered federal assistance to a New Hampshire town following a large and destructive fire. Throughout the nineteenth and early twentieth centuries, the US Congress continued to pass legislation to allow aid for Americans affected by hurricanes, earthquakes, floods, droughts, and other natural disasters.

The federal response to natural disasters began to change by the 1930s. The Reconstruction Finance Corporation was tasked with making loans to repair and reconstruct certain public facilities following natural disasters. In 1934 the Bureau of Public Roads was made responsible for funding the repair of highways and bridges damaged by natural disasters. The Flood Control Act was passed during this period, which gave the US Army Corps of Engineers greater authority to implement flood control projects.

With disaster assistance spread over several agencies in the federal government, there was a great deal of cooperation needed between them to provide a coordinated and effective response.

It became clear to officials that these responsibilities should be brought together under the supervision of one department.

In 1973 the Federal Disaster Assistance Administration was established within the Department of Housing and Urban Development (HUD). It was anticipated that the new agency would effectively coordinate and oversee major federal response and recovery operations to large-scale natural disasters, hazards, and emergencies; however, that is not how it worked in practice. The federal government's emergency and disaster activities were still piecemeal, involving multiple federal agencies involved in some aspect of any emergency response. In addition, there were parallel programs and policies existing at the state and local level, which confused and complicated federal disaster relief efforts. It was clear that reforms had to be made to resolve the numerous inefficiencies and problems within the US federal bureaucracy.

In 1979 President Jimmy Carter issued an executive order creating FEMA. This brought together many of the separate disaster-related responsibilities under the umbrella of one agency. FEMA underwent a major reform in the 1990s, when director James L. Witt streamlined disaster relief and recovery operations and prioritized preparedness and disaster relief.

The terrorist attacks of September 11, 2001, resulted in the creation of the Department of Homeland Security in 2003. FEMA was subsumed under the new department, which implemented a coordinated approach to national security from terrorism, natural disasters, and other emergencies.

Another major reform to FEMA took place in 2006, when President George W. Bush signed into law the Post-Katrina Emergency Management Reform Act. This piece of legislation was passed to address gaps that became apparent in the federal response to Hurricane Katrina in August 2005, the most devastating natural disaster in US history.

The debate over FEMA's role in disaster relief and emergency services is one of the topics discussed in the following chapter, which examines the government's role in natural disaster relief. Other subjects explored in the chapter include the responsibility of states and individuals and the consequences of utilizing multinational troops in disaster zones.

"Natural disasters ... are a much-needed reminder of just how important a functional big government turns out to be to our survival."

The US Government Must Be Responsible for Disaster Relief and Risk Reduction

Christian Parenti

In the following viewpoint, the author points out that the increasing number of natural disasters and extreme weather events caused by global warming will force many people to reassess their opinion of the role of big government in American life. He argues that events such as Hurricane Irene in 2011 remind Americans that big government plays an essential role in relief and rebuilding after destructive natural disasters. He asserts that if one were to look at the history of the United States, one would see that government has always taken a lead role in developing the country's infrastructure and economy. In the face of the devastating impact that climate change will have on the world's extreme weather patterns, he concludes, big government will become even more essential to the nation's survival and economic success. Christian Parenti is an author and contributing editor for the Nation.

As you read, consider the following questions:
1. According to the World Bank as cited by Parenti, what was the estimated damage of the 2011 flooding in Thailand?
2. What percentage of all flood insurance in the United States does the author say comes from the National Flood Insurance program?
3. According to Parenti, how many Major Disaster Declarations were made by the federal government in 2011?

Look back on 2011 and you'll notice a destructive trail of extreme weather slashing through the year. In Texas, it was the driest year ever recorded. An epic drought there killed half a billion trees, touched off wildfires that burned four million acres, and destroyed or damaged thousands of homes and buildings. The costs to agriculture, particularly the cotton and cattle businesses, are estimated at $5.2 billion—and keep in mind that, in a winter breaking all sorts of records for warmth, the Texas drought is not yet over.

In August, the East Coast had a close brush with calamity in the form of Hurricane Irene. Luckily, that storm had spent most of its energy by the time it hit land near New York City. Nonetheless, its rains did at least $7 billion worth of damage, putting it just below the $7.2 billion worth of chaos caused by Katrina back in 2005.

Across the planet the story was similar. Wildfires consumed large swaths of Chile. Colombia suffered its second year of endless rain, causing an estimated $2 billion in damage. In Brazil, the life-giving Amazon River was running low due to drought. Northern Mexico is still suffering from its worst drought in 70 years. Flooding in the Thai capital, Bangkok, killed over 500 and displaced or damaged the property of 12 million others, while ruining some of the world's largest industrial parks. The World Bank estimates the damage in Thailand at a mind-boggling $45 billion, making it one of the most expensive disasters ever. And that's just to start a 2011 extreme-weather list, not to end it.

The Role of Government

Such calamities, devastating for those affected, have important implications for how we think about the role of government in our future. During natural disasters, society regularly turns to the state for help, which means such immediate crises are a much-needed reminder of just how important a functional big government turns out to be to our survival.

These days, big government gets big press attention—none of it anything but terrible. In the United States, especially in an election year, it's become fashionable to beat up on the public sector and all things governmental (except the military). The Right does it nonstop. All their talking points disparage the role of an oversized federal government. Anti-tax zealot Grover Norquist famously set the tone for this assault. "I'm not in favor of abolishing the government," he said. "I just want to shrink it down to the size where we can drown it in the bathtub." He has managed to get 235 members of the House of Representatives and 41 members of the Senate to sign his "Taxpayer Protection Pledge" and thereby swear never, under any circumstances, to raise taxes.

By now, this viewpoint has taken on the aura of folk wisdom, as if the essence of democracy were to hate government. Even many on the Left now regularly dismiss government as nothing but oversized, wasteful, bureaucratic, corrupt, and oppressive, without giving serious consideration to how essential it may be to our lives.

Only Government Can Effectively Help

But don't expect the present "consensus" to last. Global warming and the freaky, increasingly extreme weather that will accompany it is going to change all that. After all, there is only one institution that actually has the capacity to deal with multibillion-dollar natural disasters on an increasingly routine basis. Private security firms won't help your flooded or tornado-struck town. Private insurance companies are systematically withdrawing coverage from vulnerable coastal areas. Voluntary community groups, churches, anarchist affinity groups—each may prove helpful in limited ways, but for better or worse, only government has the capital and capacity to deal with the catastrophic implications of climate change.

Consider Hurricane Irene: as it passed through the Northeast, states mobilized more than 100,000 National Guard troops. New York City opened 78 public emergency shelters prepared to house up to 70,000 people. In my home state, Vermont, where the storm devastated the landscape, destroying or damaging 200 bridges, more than 500 miles of road, and 100 miles of railroad, the National Guard airlifted in free food, water, diapers, baby formula, medicine, and tarps to thousands of desperate Vermonters trapped in 13 stranded towns—all free of charge to the victims of the storm.

The damage to Vermont was estimated at up to $1 billion. Yet the state only has 621,000 residents, so it could never have raised all the money needed to rebuild alone. Vermont businesses, individuals, and foundations have donated at least $4 million, possibly up to $6 million in assistance, an impressive figure, but not a fraction of what was needed. The state government immediately released $24 million in funds, crucial to getting its system of roads rebuilt and functioning, but again that was a drop in the bucket, given the level of damage. A little-known state-owned bank, the Vermont Municipal Bond Bank, also offered low-interest, low-collateral loans to towns to aid reconstruction efforts. But without federal money, which covered 80% to 100% of the costs of rebuilding many Vermont roads, the state would still be an economic basket case. Without aid from Washington, the transportation network might have taken years to recover.

Flood Insurance

As for flood insurance, the federal government is pretty much the only place to get it. The National Flood Insurance Program has written 5.5 million policies in more than 21,000 communities covering $1.2 trillion worth of property. As for the vaunted private market, for-profit insurance companies write between 180,000 and 200,000 policies in a given year. In other words, that is less than 5% of all flood insurance in the United States. This federally subsidized program underwrites the other 95%. Without such insurance, it's not complicated: many waterlogged victims of 2011, whether from record Midwestern floods or Hurricane Irene, would simply have no money to rebuild.

Or consider sweltering Texas. In 2011, firefighters responded to 23,519 fires. In all, 2,742 homes were destroyed by out-of-control wildfires. But government action saved 34,756 other homes. So you decide: Was this another case of wasteful government intervention in the marketplace, or an extremely efficient use of resources?

Facing Snowpocalypse

The early years of this century have already offered a number of examples of how disastrous too little government can be in the face of natural disaster, Katrina-inundated New Orleans in 2005 being perhaps the quintessential case.

There are, however, other less noted examples that nonetheless helped concentrate the minds of government planners. For example, in the early spring of 2011, a massive blizzard hit New York City. Dubbed "Snowmageddon" and "Snowpocalypse," the storm arrived in the midst of tense statewide budget negotiations, and a nationwide assault on state workers (and their pensions).

In New York, Mayor Mike Bloomberg was pushing for cuts to the sanitation department budget. As the snow piled up, the people tasked with removing it—sanitation workers—failed to appear in sufficient numbers. As the city ground to a halt, New Yorkers were left to fend for themselves with nothing but shovels,

The Early History of FEMA

President [Jimmy] Carter's 1979 executive order merged many of the separate disaster-related responsibilities into the Federal Emergency Management Agency (FEMA). Among other agencies, FEMA absorbed: the Federal Insurance Administration, the National Fire Prevention and Control Administration, the National Weather Service Community Preparedness Program, the Federal Preparedness Agency of the General Services Administration and the Federal Disaster Assistance Administration activities from HUD [Department of Housing and Urban Development]. Civil defense responsibilities were also transferred to the new agency from the Defense Department's Defense Civil Preparedness Agency.

John Macy was named as FEMA's first director. Macy emphasized the similarities between natural hazards preparedness and the civil defense activities. FEMA began development of an Integrated Emergency Management System with an all-hazards approach that included "direction, control and warning systems which are common to the full range of emergencies from small isolated events to the ultimate emergency—war." . . .

Early disasters and emergencies included the contamination of Love Canal, the Cuban refugee crisis and the accident at the Three Mile Island nuclear power plant. Later, the Loma Prieta Earthquake in 1989 and Hurricane Andrew in 1992 focused major national attention on FEMA. In 1993, President Clinton nominated James L. Witt as the new FEMA director. . . . The end of the cold war . . . allowed Witt to redirect more of FEMA's limited resources from civil defense into disaster relief, recovery and mitigation programs.

"FEMA History," FEMA, August 11, 2010.
www.fema.gov.

their cars, doorways, stores, roads all hopelessly buried. Chaos ensued. Though nowhere near as destructive as Katrina, the storm became a case study in too little governance and the all-too-distinct limits of "self-reliance" when nature runs amuck. In the week that followed, even the rich were stranded amid the mounting heaps of snow and uncollected garbage.

A New Perspective

Mayor Bloomberg emerged from the debacle chastened, even though he accused the union of staging a soft strike, a work-to-rule-style slowdown that held the snowbound city hostage. The union denied engaging in any such illegal actions. Whatever the case, the blizzard focused thinking locally on the nature of public workers. It suddenly made sanitation workers less invisible and forced a set of questions: Are public workers really "union fat cats" with "sinecures" gorging at the public trough? Or are they as essential to the basic functions of the city as white blood cells to the health of the human body? Clearly, in snowbound New York it was the latter. No sanitation workers and your city instantly turns chaotic and fills with garbage, leaving street after street lined with the stuff.

More broadly the question raised was: Can an individual, a town, a city, even a state really "go it alone" when the weather turns genuinely threatening? Briefly, all the union bashing and attacks on the public sector that had marked that year's state-level budget debates began to sound unhinged.

In the Big Apple at least, when Irene came calling that August, Mayor Bloomberg was ready. He wasn't dissing or scolding unions. He wasn't whining about the cost of running a government. He embraced planning, the public sector, public workers, and coordinated collective action. His administration took unprecedented steps like shutting down the subway and moving its trains to higher ground. Good thing they did. Several low-lying subway yards flooded. Had trains been parked there, many millions in public capital might have been lost or damaged.

A Secret History

When thinking about the forces of nature and the nature of infrastructure, a slightly longer view of history is instructive. And here's where to start: in the U.S., despite its official pro-market myths, government has always been the main force behind the development of a national infrastructure, and so of the country's overall economic prosperity.

One can trace the origins of state participation in the economy back to at least the founding of the republic: from Alexander Hamilton's First Bank of the United States, which refloated the entire post-revolutionary economy when it bought otherwise worthless colonial debts at face value; to Henry Clay's half-realized program of public investment and planning called the American System; to the New York State–funded Erie Canal, which made the future Big Apple the economic focus of the eastern seaboard; to the railroads, built on government land grants, that took the economy west and tied the nation together; to New Deal programs that helped pull the country out of the Great Depression and built much of the infrastructure we still use, like the Hoover Dam, scores of major bridges, hospitals, schools, and so on; to the government-funded and sponsored interstate highway system launched in the late 1950s; to the similarly funded space race, and beyond. It's simple enough: big government investments (and thus big government) has been central to the remarkable economic dynamism of the country.

Government has created roads, highways, railways, ports, the postal system, inland waterways, universities, and telecommunications systems. Government-funded R&D [research and development], as well as the buying patterns of government agencies—(alas!) both often connected to war and war-making plans—have driven innovation in everything from textiles and shipbuilding to telecoms, medicine, and high-tech breakthroughs of all sorts. Individuals invent technology, but in the United States it is almost always public money that brings the technology to scale, be it in aeronautics, medicine, computers, or agriculture.

The Essential Role of Government

Without constant government planning and subsidies, American capitalism simply could not have developed as it did, making ours the world's largest economy. Yes, the entrepreneurs we are taught to venerate have been key to all this, but dig a little deeper and you soon find that most of their oil was on public lands, their technology nurtured or invented thanks to government-sponsored R&D, or supported by excellent public infrastructure and the possibility of hiring well-educated workers produced by a heavily subsidized higher-education system. Just to cite one recent example, the now-familiar Siri voice-activated command system on the new iPhone is based on—brace yourself—government-developed technology.

And here's a curious thing: everybody more or less knows all this and yet it is almost never acknowledged. If one were to write the secret history of free enterprise in the United States, one would have to acknowledge that it has always been and remains at least a little bit socialist. However, it's not considered proper to discuss government planning in open, realistic, and mature terms, so we fail to talk about what government could—or rather, must—do to help us meet the future of climate change.

The onset of ever more extreme and repeated weather events is likely to change how we think about the role of the state. But attitudes toward the Federal Emergency Management Agency (FEMA), which stands behind state and local disaster responses, suggest that we're hardly at that moment yet. In late 2011, with Americans beleaguered by weather disasters, FEMA came under attack from congressional Republicans, eager to starve it of funds. One look at FEMA explains why.

Yes, when George W. Bush put an unqualified playboy at its helm, the agency dealt disastrously with Hurricane Katrina back in 2005. Under better leadership, however, it has been anything but the sinister apparatus of repression portrayed by legions of rightists and conspiracy theorists. FEMA is, in fact, an eminently effective mechanism for planning focused on the public good, not private profit, a form of public insurance and public assistance for Americans struck by disaster. Every year FEMA gives hundreds of millions of dollars to local firefighters and first responders, as well as victims dealing with the aftershock of floods, fires, and the other calamities associated with extreme weather events.

The Disaster Cycle

The agency's work is structured around what it calls "the disaster life cycle"—the process through which emergency managers prepare for, respond to, and help others recover from and reduce the risk of disasters. More concretely, FEMA's services include training, planning, coordinating, and funding state and local disaster managers and first responders, grant-making to local governments, institutions, and individuals, and direct emergency assistance that ranges from psychological counseling and medical aid to emergency unemployment benefits. FEMA also subsidizes long-term rebuilding and planning efforts by communities affected by disasters. In other words, it actually represents an excellent use of your tax dollars to provide services aimed at restoring local economic health and so the tax base. The anti-government Right hates FEMA for the same reason that they hate Social Security—because it works!

As it happens, thanks in part to the congressional GOP's [Republican Party's] sabotage efforts, thousands of FEMA's long-term recovery projects are now on hold, while the cash-strapped agency shifts its resources to deal with only the most immediate crises. This represents a dangerous trend, given what historical statistics tell us about our future. In recent decades, the number of Major Disaster Declarations by the federal government has been escalating sharply: only 12 in 1961, 17 in 1971, 15 in 1981, 43 in 1991, and in 2011—99! As a result, just when Hurricane

Irene bore down on the East Coast, FEMA's disaster relief fund had already been depleted from $2.4 billion as the year began to a mere $792 million.

A Mixed Economy

Like it or not, government is a huge part of our economy. Altogether, federal, state, and local government activity—that is collecting fees, taxing, borrowing and then spending on wages, procurement, contracting, grant-making, subsidies and aid—constitutes about 35% of the gross domestic product. You could say that we already live in a somewhat "mixed economy": that is, an economy that fundamentally combines private and public economic activity.

The intensification of climate change means that we need to acknowledge the chaotic future we face and start planning for it. Think of what's coming, if you will, as a kind of storm socialism.

After all, climate scientists believe that atmospheric concentrations of carbon dioxide beyond 350 parts-per-million (ppm) could set off compounding feedback loops and so lock us into runaway climate change. We are already at 392 ppm. Even if we stopped burning all fossil fuels immediately, the disruptive effect of accumulated CO_2 in the atmosphere is guaranteed to hammer us for decades. In other words, according to the best-case scenario, we face decades of increasingly chaotic and violent weather.

In the face of an unraveling climate system, there is no way that private enterprise alone will meet the threat. And though small "d" democracy and "community" may be key parts of a strong, functional, and fair society, volunteerism and "self-organization" alone will prove as incapable as private enterprise in responding to the massive challenges now beginning to unfold.

To adapt to climate change will mean coming together on a large scale and mobilizing society's full range of resources. In other words, Big Storms require Big Government. Who else will save stranded climate refugees, or protect and rebuild infrastructure, or coordinate rescue efforts and plan out the flow and allocation of resources?

It will be government that does these tasks or they will not be done at all.

> *"The United States needs to return to a decentralized disaster response framework in which states . . . bear the cost of disasters that occur in their own jurisdictions."*

States Should Be Responsible for Disaster Relief, Not the US Government

Matt Mayer, David C. John, and James Jay Carafano

In the following viewpoint, three researchers urge Congress to ignore calls to adopt a federal catastrophic hurricane (CAT) fund, which would provide government insurance to those in hurricane-prone regions. They oppose the plan because they believe private insurance companies have enough resources to deal with the matter, a federal CAT fund would further distort the property and casualty market, and the American people do not need another inefficient big-government program. Matt Mayer is an author, educator, and a visiting fellow at the Heritage Foundation, and David C. John and James Jay Carafano are senior research fellows at the Heritage Foundation.

As you read, consider the following questions:
1. According to the authors, what was the most expensive natural disaster in US history?
2. How many US states do Mayer, John, and Carafano say face a potential and predictable risk of a nationally catastrophic natural disaster?
3. How long do the authors say that the US government has thrived without a CAT fund?

A long with the winds, rain, and storm surges of Hurricane Katrina came a cacophony of voices urging Congress to adopt a catastrophic hurricane fund (CAT fund). A CAT fund, like the bankrupt and highly inefficient National Flood Insurance Program (NFIP), would provide government insurance to homeowners and businesses to protect against the next catastrophic hurricane. Lost in the chorus of doomsayers is the inconvenient fact that Hurricane Katrina—the most expensive natural disaster in American history—did not bankrupt the insurance industry. Unlike the current Wall Street financial crisis, the industry did not even require a federal bailout.

Inconvenient Facts

From 1970 to 2006, America experienced 23 insured catastrophic losses due to natural disasters or terrorism ranging from $45 billion down to $1.993 billion (in 2005 dollars). These included 15 hurricanes, one earthquake, and the terrorist attacks on September 11, 2001. Only four caused insured losses greater than $15 billion. Over the past 18 years [1991–2009], only five years have seen insured catastrophic losses in excess of $15 billion: $22.9 billion in 1992 (Hurricane Andrew); $16.9 billion in 1994 (Northridge earthquake); $26.5 billion in 2001 (9/11 terrorist attacks); $27.5 billion in 2004 (Hurricanes Frances, Charley, Ivan, and Jeanne); and $61.9 billion in 2005 (Hurricanes Katrina, Rita, and Wilma).

As one expert noted, the insurance "industry held about $400 billion in equity capital and collected premiums of about

$440 billion" in 2004. While only 12 percent of those funds represented premiums from homeowners insurance, that still amounts to $52.8 billion in yearly premiums. Assuming that actuarially unsound state rate caps are lifted and insurance companies take a tighter approach to paying homeowners claims, insurance companies appear easily capable of dealing with all but the most catastrophic natural disasters—they have already dealt with the most catastrophic disaster to date.

A Different Approach

Despite these inconvenient facts, proponents of a CAT fund continue to push for another federal program that would further distort the property and casualty (P&C) insurance market. As with many federal proposals, a CAT fund started small as a hurricane-centric idea, but California's congressional delegation would likely seek to add earthquakes to any proposed legislation. Yet no matter what is covered, a CAT fund would federalize even more of America's natural disaster response and spread the risks willingly accepted by a minority of taxpayers to a majority of taxpayers who live far away from routine hurricane and earthquake activity. Common sense demands a different approach.

In 2007, one CAT fund proposal, The Homeowners Defense Act (H.R. 3355), embodied many of the worst characteristics of CAT funds. It would have made it easier to create a federal government subsidy of P&C coverage for natural disasters. The bill would also have made it easier for individual states to create unrealistic disaster insurance programs, with underpriced policies, by creating a federal loan fund to cover losses suffered by those programs. Although states are already empowered to create such consortiums, H.R. 3355 would have granted this consortium a federal charter that would appear to extend a federal guarantee to the bonds issued by the group, when in fact no such guarantee would have existed. This false federal imprimatur could have increased pressure for a federal bailout following the inevitable disaster.

Five Principles of Reform

Rather than trying to second-guess the collective wisdom of the private sector, this paper establishes five principles that should guide any catastrophic natural disaster insurance reform. Underpinning these principles is the belief that the private sector, state governments, and—as a last resort—the federal government could take many actions short of creating a CAT fund that would provide greater stability to the insurance market at a lower cost to most taxpayers.

Strictly Enforced Parameters

Principle #1: Catastrophic should mean nationally catastrophic. As noted in previous papers over the past 16 years, the disaster response community has explicitly and implicitly reduced the threshold of what qualifies as a natural disaster eligible for a federal declaration. This "defining disaster down" approach is largely driven by the 75 percent or more cost-share provision that Congress included in the 1988 Robert T. Stafford Disaster Relief and Emergency Assistance Act (Stafford Act). This helps to explain why disaster declarations are granted months *after* the events when there are simply no emergencies and the events clearly had been handled without federal involvement.

In the Stafford Act, the express threshold for a declaration is a disaster "of such severity and magnitude that effective response is beyond the capabilities of the State and the affected local governments and that Federal assistance is necessary." Despite this clear requirement, the Federal Emergency Management Agency (FEMA) has approved disaster declarations for many natural disasters that historically and factually were not beyond the capabilities of states and localities. Other than hurricanes, earthquakes, volcanic eruptions, and tsunamis, most natural disasters in America lack the potential to meet the Stafford Act definition. Even most hurricanes, earthquakes, volcanic eruptions, and tsunamis do not meet the Stafford Act requirement.

Federal Emergency Declarations by Presidential Administration

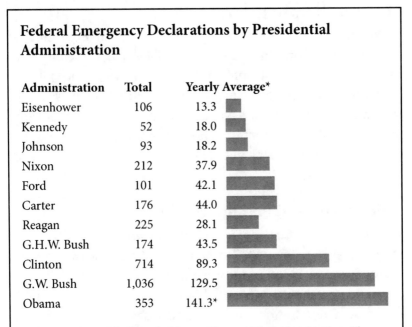

Administration	Total	Yearly Average*	
Eisenhower	106	13.3	
Kennedy	52	18.0	
Johnson	93	18.2	
Nixon	212	37.9	
Ford	101	42.1	
Carter	176	44.0	
Reagan	225	28.1	
G.H.W. Bush	174	43.5	
Clinton	714	89.3	
G.W. Bush	1,036	129.5	
Obama	353	141.3*	

* Figures are prorated for Kennedy, Johnson, Nixon, and Ford Administrations. Obama Administration figures are projected based on data through July 11, 2011.

Note: Annual totals may not add up to presidential totals during the same time period due to the January 20 inauguration date.

TAKEN FROM: The Heritage Foundation, "FEMA Declarations by Administration," August 31, 2011. www.heritage.org.

Of course, that does not mean that a particular natural disaster is not "catastrophic" for a particular community. It simply means that most natural disasters occur within confined geographic areas and that states and localities can handle them without federal involvement. At least, they should be and used to be before the [Bill] Clinton and [George W.] Bush Administrations federalized more and more of America's disaster response activities, giving states and localities an incentive to reduce their own investment in disaster response capabilities.

As noted above, most natural disasters over the past 18 years have caused insured losses of less than $15 billion. Every one of the natural disasters occurred primarily in an 11-state area. Most of the 11 states have yearly budgets well in excess of $15 billion, so they should be capable of crafting state-based programs to handle catastrophic natural disasters, including raising taxes when necessary to fund a state-based CAT fund.

Recommendations for Decentralization

Fundamentally, the United States needs to return to a decentralized disaster response framework in which states and the people living in the states bear the cost of disasters that occur in their own jurisdictions.

Therefore, the most critical principle is that for FEMA disaster declarations "catastrophic" must actually mean nationally catastrophic. Toward this end, Congress should:

- Amend the Stafford Act to limit eligibility for FEMA disaster declarations to hurricanes, earthquakes, volcanic eruptions, and tsunamis, explicitly excluding other natural disasters;
- Insert severity and magnitude thresholds for these four types of disasters so that only those that are truly national emergencies qualify for federal involvement;
- Adopt a high economic threshold requirement for any program that is created to prevent a national catastrophic natural disaster from bankrupting the insurance industry. For example, one insurance company suggested a $125 billion trigger for a lender-of-last-resort program.

Such a trigger is necessary given the federal tendency to spend the money by expanding eligibility downward. This tendency will increase if paid premiums piled up during years without any eligible events. Accountability needs to be returned to the governors and the people.

Risk Assumers Should Also Bear Risk

Principle #2: Those who assume the risk should bear the risk.
We possess at least 55 years of actuarial data on where and when natural disasters occur. Roughly 11 states face a potential and predictable risk of a nationally catastrophic natural disaster. These states and the corresponding potential disasters are:

Texas	hurricane
Louisiana	hurricane
Alabama	hurricane
Mississippi	hurricane
Florida	hurricane
Georgia	hurricane
South Carolina	hurricane
North Carolina	hurricane
California	earthquake
Washington	volcanic eruption
Hawaii	tsunami, volcanic eruption

Of course, other states could experience a nationally catastrophic natural disaster, but the frequency of such events is very low, which minimizes the assumption-of-the-risk concept. Thus, individuals and businesses living in those places should not face steeper insurance rates because the probability of such an event is low, hard to price, and impossible to predict. For example, a catastrophic hurricane could hit New York and Connecticut, but such an event may not happen for many years, if at all.[1] Therefore, individuals living in those states cannot be held to be placing themselves at risk of such a low-probability event. If such a catastrophe occurred, a state-based program paid for by its taxpayers to deal with the economic impact should take precedence over a federal program paid for by taxpayers outside of that state.

In contrast, as the much-referenced map developed by Risk Management Solutions vividly illustrates, only a handful of states are predictably at risk of a nationally catastrophic natural disaster. Individuals and businesses in those states, especially in jurisdictions close to the coast and along the San Andreas Fault Line, have unquestionably assumed the risk of a catastrophic natural disaster.

This is especially true for the individuals and businesses that have moved to those jurisdictions over the past two decades. Six of the 11 states have experienced population growth above the national average from 1990 to 2007. With the influx in population and attendant development, the cost of natural disasters has steadily increased.

Rate Caps Pose a Moral Hazard

To attract and keep these individuals and businesses, states have imposed rate caps to prevent insurance companies from charging actuarially sound P&C insurance rates. These state rate caps have prevented insurance companies from securing sufficient capital reserves and, more troubling, indirectly spread the cost of their known risks to other, less risk-prone states. Hence, the rate caps in these 11 states have resulted in the other 39 states—many of which lost population, businesses, and tax revenue to the 11 states—subsidizing the cost of living in those 11 states. Such a moral hazard has disconnected the risk from those who willingly assumed the risk and enjoy the benefits of living in a warmer and more scenic place.

In nine of the 11 states, not including Florida and California, a majority of their populations and land areas are a safe distance away from the coast, thereby providing a large pool of individuals and businesses that can diversify the risk of insuring the coastal areas. At least those individuals who live in the high-risk states directly benefit from their robust and viable coastal communities. However, it is a bit harder to see how someone living in the Upper Peninsula of Michigan should bear the cost of insuring high-risk coastal or fault-line communities.

Given these realities, individuals and businesses in the 39 lower-risk states should not pay higher P&C insurance rates or pay higher federal taxes to subsidize the living costs of those individuals and business that choose to locate in the 11 high-risk states. This is especially true given the irresponsible coastal and fault line development over the past two decades in spite of the high risks.

Injecting Competition into the Mix

Furthermore, Florida and Texas heavily promote their lack of a state income tax to encourage individuals and businesses to relocate into their jurisdictions. Low-risk states ought to be equally justified in promoting their significantly lower P&C insurance rates to retain or attract the same individuals and businesses. Since owning a home is the single largest cost-of-living expense, substantially lower P&C rates would equate to a discernible advantage. If competition is good in tax policy, then competition among the states in P&C insurance rates should also be good. Yet it is taken almost as gospel that high-risk states should not be required to charge actuarially sound P&C insurance rates. This belief should be rejected because it ignores reality.

It is axiomatic that public policy should place the full burden of risk on those who assume that risk. States need to eliminate arbitrary rate caps on P&C insurance so that the insured parties pay fully for the risk of their actions, thereby allowing insurance companies to acquire capital reserves sufficient to deal with most, if not all, natural disasters.

Five Requirements

Principle #3: State eligibility should depend on meeting five requirements. To be eligible for any federal catastrophic natural disaster program, a state should meet five requirements:

1. *No rate caps.* The state must eliminate rate caps and permit insurance companies to charge actuarially sound P&C insurance rates. Before receiving federal taxpayer funds, the state must have allowed insurance companies the op-

portunity to earn capital reserves sufficient to meet any obligations. Otherwise, taxpayers in other states are forced to subsidize the high-risk state's irresponsible behavior. The decision by State Farm, the largest P&C insurer in Florida, to stop offering coverage in Florida because the state refuses to let it charge an actuarially sound rate demonstrates that this issue is not theoretical.

2. *Sound building codes.* The state must enact and enforce sound building codes that minimize damage from known natural disaster risks. Due to the aggressive development in high-risk areas, the costs of natural disasters have increased substantially. Therefore, it makes eminent sense to require states to enact and enforce sound building codes known to mitigate the vulnerabilities and consequences of known risks.

3. *No redevelopment of disaster-prone areas.* The state must prohibit redevelopment of disaster-prone areas unless the U.S. Army Corps of Engineers has approved the mitigation action taken to prevent repetitive losses and the private sector insurance market has ascertained, through offering rate-cap-free P&C policies, that the mitigation action has eliminated or minimized the repetitive loss issue. As learned from the NFIP, the only outcome that can be expected from rebuilding in a known flood zone is a flooded structure. This insanity must end.

4. *Tort reform.* As important, the state must enact tort reform to eliminate or significantly reduce the frivolous lawsuits by overzealous lawyers seeking to capitalize on sensational headlines and public sympathy following a natural disaster. In most cases, the insurance companies win such lawsuits. Nonetheless, insurance companies must spend millions of dollars defending insurance contracts. In some cases, insurance companies settle to avoid negative publicity or a stacked deck in "jackpot"

jurisdictions. Baseless lawsuits only drive up the cost of P&C policies for consumers.

5. *Mandated P&C insurance.* Finally, states must require individuals and businesses in known hurricane, earthquake, and flood zones to purchase P&C insurance, including state-based earthquake and hurricane insurance and federal flood insurance. Such a mandate will increase the capital reserves of insurance companies and the liquidity of government insurance programs.

Opt-in Only

Principle 4: State participation should be opt-in only. One of the greatest aspects of American democracy is its adherence to federalism. As U.S. Supreme Court Justice Louis Brandeis noted many years ago, America has its "laborator[ies]" of democracy that constantly seek ways to meet objectives more efficiently and more effectively. As the Risk Management Solutions map illustrates, most states do not face a predictable catastrophic natural disaster risk. Forcing those states to join a catastrophic natural disaster program is inherently unfair and violates U.S. federalist principles. Hence, governors and state legislatures—not the federal government—should decide whether or not their individual states will opt into any catastrophic natural disaster program and its higher P&C rates.

Tax Laws Should Be Changed

Principle 5: Tax and accounting policies must permit insurance and reinsurance companies to retain sufficient capital reserves. Before launching another federal program, Congress should amend existing tax laws that prevent insurance and reinsurance companies from taking tax deductions for capital reserves. Concomitant with tax reform, the accounting industry should alter generally accepted accounting principles to permit insurance and reinsurance companies to establish reserves for potential catastrophes. These two changes would provide incentives for those companies to establish larger capital reserves for potential catastrophic natural disasters, thereby reducing the need for government assistance.

Are These Principles Enough?

These five principles are a good start, but even they may not be enough to justify passage of a CAT fund. Experience has shown that both states and insurance companies have used CAT funds and similar insurance programs to shift risk to the federal government that should be retained by insurance companies. They have used such programs to obtain back-door federal subsidies for state property insurance and reinsurance systems, which are designed more to help taxpayers avoid paying insurance rates than reflect the true risk to their properties.

State governments are free to develop irresponsible property insurance programs provided that they and their citizens understand that they must bear the consequences. CAT funds that create a direct federal loan program to provide federal "bridge loans" to cover losses to state reinsurance programs when natural disaster claims exceed the state funds' assets need special scrutiny. Experience with the federal flood insurance program shows that once federal loans reach a significant level, there will be an immediate attempt to persuade the government to forgive them. At that point, the "bridge loan" program becomes a back-door approach for the federal government to assume much of the risk for property losses caused by hurricanes and similar disasters.

Limiting Government

Over the past six months [November 2008–April 2009], we have witnessed an unprecedented expansion of federal control, power, spending, and deficits. As we are quickly learning, federal expansion comes at a steep price and with the entire baggage of waste, fraud, and abuse that is expected with monolithic, opaque federal action. It is high time that America steps back from this dangerous precipice before the government structure is changed wholly beyond the one designed by the Founding Fathers in the Constitution.

Those who sound the clarion call for federalizing more disasters would do well to read the Constitution, *The Federalist Papers*, and *The Heritage Guide to the Constitution*. As President Calvin Coolidge remarked on the 150th Anniversary of the Declaration of Independence, "It is not so much then for the purpose of undertaking to proclaim new theories and principles that this annual celebration is maintained, but rather to reaffirm and re-establish those old theories and principles which time and the unerring logic of events have demonstrated to be sound." History has repeatedly shown that federalization is rarely the path to a better tomorrow.

The U.S. has thrived for 223 years without a federal CAT fund. Other than irresponsible government action, a lack of leadership and accountability, and a federally incented policy of ignoring risk, nothing is preventing states from freeing insurance companies to charge actuarially sound P&C insurance rates and citizens from bearing the costs of the risks they assume.

Nothing but politics, that is.

Note

1. Since this viewpoint was originally published, two devastating hurricanes have hit this part of the United States: Irene in 2011 and Sandy in 2012.

"*Americans, regardless of race, color,*
or creed, will gladly contribute a few
dollars to help those communities that
have suffered from natural disasters."

American Citizens Should Handle Disaster Relief and Not Big Government

Bruce Walker

In the following viewpoint, a writer argues that Americans should not rely on government disaster relief programs in the wake of natural disasters. Instead, he maintains, they should draw from private charities and the generosity of volunteers, a system that has proven successful after recent destructive tornadoes in Oklahoma and Arkansas. He contends that the American people will instinctually open their hearts, homes, and wallets to communities that have been destroyed by natural disasters. Therefore, he concludes, Americans should reject the "social lecturing by institutional or government bureaucrats" as well as government relief programs that only expand big government. Bruce Walker is a contributor to New American.

As you read, consider the following questions:

1. According to Walker, how many homeowners in Pulaski, Virginia, lost their homes in a recent tornado?
2. What percentage of firefighters in America does the author say are volunteer firefighters and emergency responders?
3. Who provided shelter and food for the victims of the tornado in Tushka, Oklahoma, as cited by Walker?

Tornadoes wreaked havoc in Oklahoma and Arkansas, killing several people. This is the sort of very real human tragedy that is not suspect to free and thinking minds. Human life, indeed, human history has been full of disasters that destroy property and kill people.

The Role of Private Charities

Reporters who go to areas of natural disasters have no motive beyond the story itself. Americans, regardless of race, color, or creed, will gladly contribute a few dollars to help those communities that have suffered from natural disasters. American charity —private giving, as opposed to state-funded social programs— has been a salient feature of a grateful people, thanking God and returning to those who have been hurt some of the blessings He has given us.

This sort of charity can be seen all over our nation every day, especially in those small businesses that are the backbone of our economy and the heart of our nation. Some poor child needs an operation and his parents cannot afford it. When you pay for your breakfast, if you could drop some coins or a dollar or two into this jar, it will help—and we do just that. People on the other side of the world suffer from a tsunami or an earthquake. We do not know them, except that, as Mother Teresa would have reminded us, they are God's beloved children. Do we aid them? Yes, and we have been doing that for a long, long time.

In fact, when we see real hardship in our city or our state, as when tornadoes come through and tear apart a small town, it is amazing just how quickly churches will dip into their budgets to help folks a hundred miles away or how many Americans will open their homes to those who suddenly do not have a home. Our instinct, our very American instinct, is to help our neighbors. This is not the result of any social lecturing by institutional or government bureaucrats. It is the natural consequence of genuine liberty in action. The help is real; it is directed as precisely as a huntsman's rifle; and it is based upon the deep and serious faith of Americans.

Private Charities Aid Disaster Victims

Consider the tornado that just savaged Pulaski, Virginia. Almost as soon as the cyclones passed, help was there—but not government help. Amy Whitaker of the Red Cross in the area said: "We've handed out water, food, cleaning supplies, clothes and even hugs." The collection site was New Life Church of the Nazarene, and Heather Harris, who is coordinating relief stated: "We are trying to combine our efforts, different churches and groups. We've got all kinds of donations coming in." Stephanie Bishop, whose family lost everything in the calamity, said: "It's been amazing. We are so blessed. We've had people coming up to the house all through the day, asking what they could do for us."

In the same small town, the Samaritan's Purse gathered volunteers who, as it said: ". . . can minister in the name of Jesus Christ to more than 300 homeowners who have lost their homes. Volunteers need to bring tarp roofs, operate chainsaws, and clear out debris. . . . Thank you for being the Hands and Feet of Jesus Christ." Faith Bible Church began serving breakfast and lunch for all victims of the disaster, as well as all state troopers and emergency responders. The church also set up a collection site for pillows, blankets, food, and related help for the victims. The Pulaski Presbyterian Church offered free lunches to everyone. The Salvation Army set up a food canteen as well.

This is not an American virtue unique to Virginia or the South. At the same time that people of faith were pouring in help

The Pulaski Tornadoes

On Friday evening April 8, 2011, several intense storms moved out of West Virginia and into southwest Virginia. Some of these storms were supercells, which contain very strong and rotating updrafts, capable of producing a full range of severe weather (damaging downburst winds, large hail, and sometimes tornadoes). One of these supercells tracked across a stationary frontal boundary, where shallow cool air had wedged down in from the northeast across much of Virginia, meeting warm, moist air pushing up from the southwest into far southwest Virginia. Supercells interacting with surface frontal boundaries can often be a recipe for tornadogenesis, and in fact that is what happened over Pulaski County. Two tornado tracks were identified in the aftermath of this storm, the first touched down in the southwest portion of the town of Pulaski at 7:33 PM and resulted in high-end EF2 damage (winds up to 125 mph), and a second tornado tracked across Interstate 81 and through the community of Draper around 7:40 PM, resulting in high-end EF1 damage (winds up to 110 mph). Fortunately, there were no fatalities during these tornadoes; however, there were several minor injuries and many residents in both communities had their homes destroyed or suffered major damage (over 50).

"Supercell Storm Results in Rare Significant Tornadoes in Pulaski County, VA, April 8th, 2011," National Weather Forecast Service, April 18, 2011.

to Pulaski, Virginia, the Valley Disaster Relief in Des Moines, Iowa came in with chainsaws and other equipment. This wholly volunteer group works with help of its own: "They said their saws aren't the only power they pack; they've got God." Dirk Roghair, a member of this group, says: "It's totally fulfilling helping someone else. We get more out of it than they do. It's a totally blessed life."

Brave and Generous Volunteers

Do statists ever wonder how, particularly in rural America, folks survive? How, for example, are homes protected from fires? An astounding 71 percent of firefighters in America are volunteer firefighters and emergency responders. These brave people risk their lives for friends, neighbors, and even strangers to save lives, protect property, and put out fires.

So what has happened in Tushka, Oklahoma, the tiny community of 345 people that was just hit by a tornado? The First Baptist Church of Atoka provided shelter for the victims. The Salvation Army began serving meals. No sooner had the news reports began and the twister swirled passed than their fellow countrymen, out of respect for God and not government, began to help.

President Obama made his pitch for bigger government recently by saying, "The America I know is generous and compassionate." He is partly right: The America that he sneered was bitter and was clinging to guns and to religion is very generous and compassionate. These volunteers are not throwing temper tantrums at the Wisconsin state capital because their benefits will not be allowed to grow exponentially. These volunteers, instead, wait to gather their riches in another place entirely, very far from the President's Washington and the havens of the elitist media.

"FEMA has dedicated itself to the mission of helping communities nationwide prepare for, respond to and recover from natural and manmade disasters."

The Federal Emergency Management Agency Provides Essential Disaster Recovery Services

Federal Emergency Management Agency

In the following viewpoint, the Federal Emergency Management Agency (FEMA) traces the essential role the federal government has had in providing disaster relief to individual and communities since 1803 and asserts that it is continuously strengthening operations to serve disaster victims and communities more quickly and effectively. FEMA asserts that it strives to improve on its core competencies, including quick access to disaster services, operational planning and preparedness, disaster logistics, and emergency communications. Its workers have, the agency explains, a broad range of experience and are dedicated to compassionately and effectively aid disaster victims when needed. FEMA was created in 1979 to coordinate the response to natural disasters within the United States.

Federal Emergency Management Agency, "FEMA: Prepared. Responsive. Committed," FEMA-B653, July, 2008. FEMA.gov. Copyright © 2008 by Federal Emergency Management Agency.

As you read, consider the following questions:
1. As of November 2007, how many presidentially declared disasters does FEMA say it has responded to?
2. How does FEMA describe its role in public disaster communications?
3. Which of its divisions does FEMA say provides prevention and preparedness programs, research, data collection, and national policy guidance?

The Congressional Act of 1803 was the earliest effort to provide disaster relief on a federal level after a fire devastated a New Hampshire town. From that point forward, assorted legislation provided disaster support. In 1979, the Federal Emergency Management Agency (FEMA) was established by an executive order, which merged many of the separate disaster-related responsibilities into a single agency. Since then, FEMA has dedicated itself to the mission of helping communities nationwide prepare for, respond to and recover from natural and manmade disasters—a mission strengthened when the agency became part of the Department of Homeland Security (DHS) in 2003. As of November 2007, FEMA has responded to more than 2,700 presidentially declared disasters.

Continuously Strengthening Operations

To serve disaster victims and communities more quickly and effectively, FEMA builds on experience, applies lessons learned and best practices from field operations, gathers feedback from many sources, and constantly strives to improve upon its operational core competencies:

Service to Disaster Victims. Responsive and compassionate care for disaster victims is FEMA's top priority. FEMA provides rapid, ready, clear and consistent access to disaster assistance to all eligible individuals and communities. The agency also is able to assist individuals with multilingual or special needs requirements.

Integrated Preparedness. FEMA works closely with federal, tribal, state and local governments, voluntary agencies, private sector partners, and the American public to ensure the nation is secured and prepared to respond to and recover from terror attacks, major disasters and other emergencies.

Operational Planning and Preparedness. Working closely with federal, tribal, state and local partners, FEMA's Operational Planners assist jurisdictions to develop planning capabilities and write area- and incident-specific operational plans that will guide local response activities.

Incident Management. With a forward-leaning posture, FEMA can respond more swiftly and decisively to all hazards with around-the-clock support. The agency continues to professionalize its workforce by training and certifying staff in emergency management skills and techniques. FEMA also works closely with external partners to improve and update standards, and support the enduring efforts of America's first responders.

Disaster Logistics. FEMA implements 21st century logistics and procurement systems to help efficiently and effectively plan, identify, track and distribute supplies needed by disaster victims, emergency responders and other users on the ground. Working with an array of public and private strategic partners, donors and pre-arranged contractors, a businesslike FEMA provides improved logistics integration and customer support.

Hazard Mitigation. FEMA works proactively to reduce the physical and financial impact of future disasters through improved risk analysis and hazard mitigation planning, risk reduction and flood insurance. FEMA helps implement effective hazard mitigation practices in order to create safer communities, promote rapid recovery from floods and other disasters, and reduce the financial impact at the federal, tribal, state and local levels.

Emergency Communications. FEMA is a leader in emergency communications by working with federal, tribal, state and local partners to establish and facilitate consistent disaster emergency communications standards, plans and capabilities. As part of this leadership role, FEMA works to forge an integrated operational link before, during and immediately after an event and is an advocate for disaster emergency communications at the national level on behalf of first responders.

Public Disaster Communications. FEMA coordinates all hazards messaging before, during and after national emergencies using three strategies: public risk communications, partnership management and employee communications. By successfully managing these elements, FEMA supports operational efforts and ensures clear, consistent and effective information for disaster victims and emergency management partners and stakeholders.

Continuity Programs. FEMA supports upgrades to and implementation of the Integrated Public Alert and Warning System. It is the lead agent for the Nation's programs in ensuring the continuity of government operations and essential functions and the endurance of our constitutional form of government in a catastrophic event.

Dedicated Leadership and Employees

FEMA staff work together with tribal, state and local emergency management personnel to prepare communities before a disaster, and to respond effectively and with care. FEMA's efforts at the national and regional levels are led by individuals with a broad range of hands-on emergency management, fire, rescue, emergency medical services, law enforcement, military and private sector experience. FEMA employees are committed to their mission of protecting lives and communities. Whether full-time, part-time, temporary, supplemental or on-call, FEMA employees serve disaster victims and communities tirelessly, with compassion and understanding.

Building a Culture of Preparedness

FEMA, through its National Preparedness Directorate and U.S. Fire Administration, provides prevention and preparedness programs, research, data collection and national policy guidance. FEMA trains emergency managers, firefighters, elected officials and other emergency responders through a variety of courses in all-hazards emergency planning and response. In addition, FEMA works through its National Emergency Training Center and Center for Domestic Preparedness, as well as with other training partners, to establish and deliver effective training and professional education programs and develop a national certification system for overall emergency management competency and expertise.

"*FEMA . . . did more to get in the way of relief [to Hurricane Katrina victims] than to actually provide and facilitate it.*"

The Federal Emergency Management Agency Impedes Rather than Aids Disaster Recovery

Ron Paul

In the following viewpoint, a US congressman states that the establishment of FEMA was based on misguided ideas of disaster relief. Although FEMA is well intentioned, he maintains, it is a bureaucratic organization beset by inefficiency and wastefulness. Instead of relying on big government to provide essential disaster relief to communities and individuals impacted by natural disasters, he contends that Americans should help themselves. In fact, the author argues, recent events show that FEMA has been a hindrance in the aftermath of Hurricane Katrina and the terrorist attacks of September 11, 2001. Representative Ron Paul of Texas has served in Congress since 1997.

Ron Paul, "We're from the Government. We're Here to Help," Congressman Ron Paul online, September 5, 2011. http://paul.house.gov.

As you read, consider the following questions:

1. According to Paul, what happened when a group of firefighters from Houston arrived to help people in New Orleans after Hurricane Katrina?
2. What does the author say happened to computer engineer Jack Harrison when he volunteered to help in the aftermath of Hurricane Katrina?
3. How many New Yorkers were taken off Manhattan by local ferries, tugboats, fishing boats, and barges after 9/11, according to Paul?

In the wake of hurricane Irene, the Federal Emergency Management Agency [FEMA] is expected to come hat in hands asking for more money from Congress. Like the rest of the government, it is broke. It has been suggested that any additional funds allocated to FEMA should come from cuts elsewhere. This seems harsh and lacking in compassion to big government advocates who do not understand economics, but I would go a step further. FEMA should never have been established. It is based on misguided ideas of disaster relief.

This seems shocking to those who have never been subjected to the secondary disaster that is the arrival of FEMA on the scene of a catastrophic event. But explaining FEMA's ineptness is not the same thing as saying no one should help people affected by disasters. Quite the opposite.

FEMA's Incompetence

Victims of disasters should get any and all help possible, and there is virtually no limit to the generosity and compassion of good American people after devastation hits. One only need to remember the outpouring after Katrina to know this is true. FEMA, however, did more to get in the way of relief than to actually provide and facilitate it. The examples are numerous. When the call was put out for volunteer firefighters, they volunteered by the thousands. It was FEMA, for reasons of control and bureaucratic ineptitude, who made sure they were not, in fact allowed to actually help. When a group of firefighters arrived from Houston, instead of being put immediately on the job, they were told to sit around and wait. After waiting for two days doing nothing, they were simply sent home. One thousand volunteer firefighters were sent to Atlanta to undergo sexual harassment training while fires actively raged in the city. The ones that remained through this stupidity were sent to escort the president around or to distribute fliers instead of putting out fires. Computer engineer Jack Harrison was told his skills were needed to rebuild technological infrastructure. After being given the runaround for about two weeks, he was misallocated as head of security on the cruise ship FEMA had leased, when he should have been using his skills to help. All manner of help was turned away or mismanaged by FEMA while people suffered and waited. Even the Red Cross had its hands tied by FEMA.

FEMA Since 9/11

It has only gotten worse since 9/11. Compare the stories of two flotillas—one after 9/11 and one after Katrina. Within an hour of the 9/11 attacks, the largest boatlift in history was organized spontaneously by locals who saw an immediate need and responded immediately. Over 500,000 terrified New Yorkers were taken off the island by ferries, tugboats, pleasure crafts, fishing boats and barges when all other access points had been shut down. A similar flotilla attempt was privately organized after Katrina. 500 boats caravanned to New Orleans to rescue patients from hospitals that were out of supplies and desperate. Unfortunately, FEMA had taken over by then and they were turned away, empty, while the patients languished, still stranded. Tragically, the Vermont Air National Guard helicopters were in Iraq when Irene hit, and they were desperately needed here.

The establishment of FEMA is symptomatic of a blind belief in big government's ability to do anything and everything for anyone and everyone. FEMA is a bureaucratic organization.

Bureaucracies, while staffed with well-meaning people, are notoriously slow and wasteful by their very nature. When people are starving, injured and dying they need speed and efficiency, yet FEMA comes along with forms and policies and rubber stamps. This sort of thing is bad enough at the DMV [Department of Motor Vehicles], but in matters of life and death where seconds count, this is just not acceptable.

True compassion would be to get FEMA out of the way.

*"[FEMA] is still poorly positioned
to respond to major emergencies . . .
because it lacks sufficient standing
within the federal bureaucracy to
garner full interagency cooperation."*

The Federal Emergency Management Agency Needs More Authority and Funding for Disaster Relief Efforts

Jessica Leval and Andrew Mener

*In the following viewpoint, the authors maintain that the Federal
Emergency Management Agency (FEMA) is poorly positioned to respond to major emergencies because it lacks sufficient authority with
the federal bureaucracy to obtain full cooperation from other agencies. They argue that FEMA's poor responses to Hurricane Andrew
in 1992 and Hurricane Katrina in 2005 led to inadequate reforms.
Jessica Leval is assistant director of the Continuity of Government
Commission (a collaboration between the American Enterprise Institute and the Brookings Institution) and a research assistant at the
American Enterprise Institute. Andrew Mener is founding chief of
the University of Pennsylvania's Emergency Medical Services.*

As you read, consider the following questions:

1. What year do the authors say that FEMA was established?
2. How much damage did Hurricane Andrew cause in 1992, according to Leval and Mener?
3. In what year did FEMA become part of the Department of Homeland Security, according to the authors?

The recent outbreak of the H1N1, or the so-called "swine flu" virus, appears mostly under control. Federal, state, and local disaster response groups have long prepared for an avian flu outbreak, a disaster comparable to a potential swine flu pandemic. And while a potential swine flu outbreak will likely be manageable due to the avian flu drills, now is an opportune time to assess the fragile state of the nation's overall disaster response system in the vast majority of other types of catastrophic disasters.

FEMA's History of Struggle

The Federal Emergency Management Agency (FEMA) sends funds to assist in disaster response, but the agency is still poorly positioned to respond to major emergencies. Despite the natural, humanitarian, and political disaster of Hurricane Katrina, FEMA cannot adequately handle large-scale emergencies because it lacks sufficient standing within the federal bureaucracy to garner full interagency cooperation. Fixing this will go a long way toward making FEMA an effective and responsive agency.

FEMA was originally created by President [Jimmy] Carter in 1979 to oversee and coordinate federal government disaster preparedness and response functions, while simultaneously allowing state and local governments to retain ultimate authority over disaster response. Federal law requires state and local authorities to first assess the damage and then submit official requests for federal aid. Only after the president has received and certified these requests can FEMA become directly involved in the disaster response efforts.

The federal government rarely assumes ultimate control of disaster response and prefers to supplement state and local resources. In the vast majority of disasters, FEMA's role has been limited to providing monetary reimbursement and logistical support to state and local agencies. While this approach has been successful in smaller-scale disasters, FEMA has failed to develop an effective national disaster plan to coordinate efforts when state resources are completely overwhelmed, in so-called "catastrophic disasters."

The problems were highlighted when category-4 storm Hurricane Andrew hit south Florida in August 1992. At the time the worst natural disaster in U.S. history, the storm killed 26 people directly and caused 39 additional deaths indirectly. State and local governments were essentially paralyzed as roughly 1.5 million people lost power and nearly 150,000 people had their phone service disrupted. The storm caused between $35 and $40 billion worth of damage, destroyed 28,000 homes, and damaged thousands of others. In the midst of the chaos, FEMA failed to coordinate the 26 federal departments and 13 "functional," or working, groups it oversees.

A Lack of Standing

The FEMA director lacked sufficient standing within the federal bureaucracy to rapidly redirect the efforts and resources of so many agencies reporting to various cabinet secretaries. Amid widespread criticism of the slow and largely ineffective federal response, President George H.W. Bush sent Secretary of Transportation Andrew Card to take control of the situation. Card was able to navigate the massive bureaucratic obstacles necessary to coordinate a national response that included so many federal, state, local, and private-sector agencies. However, because most of the 26 federal departments and 13 functional groups FEMA oversees are not located within the secretary of Transportation's jurisdiction, it is unlikely that his success stemmed from his authority as a cabinet secretary. Rather, political pressure following the initial failed response coupled with the president's clear desire to avoid additional bureaucratic failures compelled interagency cooperation.

Some of the problems highlighted during Hurricane Andrew were solved through the 2002 creation of the Department of Homeland Security, under which FEMA is now housed. In February 2003, President George W. Bush issued a directive designed to create a "single, comprehensive national incident management system." The new system promised to help achieve "full and prompt cooperation, and support" from "the heads of all federal departments and agencies" and yield greater coordination between federal, state, and local governments.

The changes were intended to ensure that homeland security concerns, including disaster preparedness, would receive sufficient standing within the federal bureaucracy to be effective, without expanding the government through the creation of a potentially controversial new cabinet-level position. But these changes were eventually proven by Hurricane Katrina to be inadequate.

The Post-Katrina Reform Act of 2006

The Post-Katrina [Emergency Management] Reform Act of 2006 was an effort to fix the nation's emergency response shortcomings. It gave the director of FEMA direct access to the president through meetings during catastrophic disasters. However, presidents must attend to many tasks frequently requiring immediate attention and must filter through constant and often conflicting advice from competing agencies and advisers. Therefore, in order for FEMA to adequately respond to the needs of a catastrophic emergency, it must be granted improved standing within the federal bureaucracy and increased access to the president in a unique way—perhaps by making the vice president, the high-level official closest to the president with more time to devote to this issue than the president could himself, the temporary co-director of FEMA only during national disasters.

The Role of the Vice President

The vice president in cooperation with the FEMA director and the secretary of Homeland Security would be better equipped to coordinate the federal disaster response during catastrophic disasters. Simply put, the vice president's seal of approval on interagency requests that require the rapid reallocation of large resources increases the likelihood that bureaucratic obstacles will be set aside during the initial phase of the federal response to a catastrophic disaster. By placing the vice president in charge of FEMA during national disasters, FEMA would be granted sufficient standing when necessary—if a disaster crosses a predetermined threshold based on perhaps the number of casualties, the size of the affected area, or if state and local officials request special assistance—but without upsetting an already delicate balance of power in the federal bureaucracy unless absolutely necessary.

James F. Miskel, former National Security Council member during the [Ronald] Reagan and George H.W. Bush administrations, and Senator Barbara Mikulski (D-Maryland) have suggested granting the vice president varying degrees of control over FEMA. However, the vice president should serve primarily as a high-level advocate, rather than micromanager of the federal disaster response. To properly prepare to step in and coordinate federal relief amid large-scale disaster, the vice president should receive information about all FEMA operations as part of his daily briefings as well as periodically meet with disaster response experts.

FEMA remains overlooked in its current positioning in the federal bureaucracy. Despite President Obama's relatively early Cabinet member selections and confirmations, he waited until early March [2009] to name a FEMA director. Obama's new director of FEMA, Craig Fugate, was only sworn in this week [in mid-May 2009]. President Obama and Congress must work to ensure that FEMA is granted appropriate standing to assure that all American resources can be quickly and efficiently redirected to save lives and relieve human suffering during the next catastrophic disaster.

> *"International military involvement in relief operations has saved countless lives in recent years, and strengthening [civil-military coordination] could further improve responses to large-scale disasters."*

Multinational Troops Can Provide Stability to Disaster Zones

James L. Schoff and Marina Travayiakis

In the following viewpoint, the authors assert that establishing a core crisis group made up of the United States, Japan, and other countries from Europe and East Asia can be invaluable in international disaster relief operations. Such a group, they maintain, would be more effective at making decisions, coordinating policies and procedures, developing a more efficient international framework for disaster response and recovery, and doing the work that needs to be done on the ground. They envision a strengthened US-Japanese collaboration to be the key to building such a coalition. James L. Schoff is director of Asia-Pacific studies at the Institute for Foreign Policy Analysis. Marina Travayiakis is a research associate at the Institute for Foreign Policy Analysis.

As you read, consider the following questions:
1. How many nations do the authors envision being in the core crisis group?
2. According to Schoff and Travayiakis, what is theater security cooperation (TSC)?
3. What does the current US-Japan Acquisition and Cross-Serving Agreement do, according to the authors?

The United States and Japan are seeking to strengthen their countries' contributions to international disaster relief efforts, and they cannot ignore the value that civil-military coordination (CMCoord) brings to these operations. International military involvement in relief operations has saved countless lives in recent years, and strengthening CMCoord could further improve responses to large-scale disasters. This experience also demonstrates, however, that organizational, legal, and cultural obstacles impede cooperation among the many actors who respond to a crisis, preventing the full realization of this CMCoord potential. The challenges are numerous and include command and control issues, information sharing, and field coordination. In addition, military support for disaster relief operations and related missions should not encroach upon the humanitarian space occupied by NGOs [nongovernmental organizations], UN agencies, and civilian government organs that are the primary tools to aid communities and nations in times of crisis.

Improving CMCoord

CMCoord and related policies are at an important stage, and improvement in this area can contribute not only to more effective relief and recovery operations, but also to greater interaction and mutual understanding among national militaries and the NGO community. Further, effective CMCoord can strengthen international and regional organizations by giving them access to more synergistic civil-military coalitions. The United States and Japan are not the only two countries engaged in this effort, but they can play a unique role by virtue of their financial power (in terms of contributions to the UN and other international organizations, and direct overseas development assistance) and their strong security relationship, which features frequent joint training exercises and a high degree of interoperability. U.S.-Japan CMCoord can create opportunities to contribute to global stability and prosperity, and at the same time it can strengthen the alliance relationship in a variety of ways that will prepare them for other important missions.

U.S.-Japan bilateral cooperation on these issues (together with other partners in the region) can help build more diverse and sophisticated alliance relationships that bring together a wider range of ministries, departments, and agencies to address common challenges of all types. This will ultimately serve to improve the ability of the alliance to work with other countries on these issues through multilateral initiatives and with international organizations. Enhancing CMCoord for disaster relief operations is a beneficial alliance exercise because:

- CMCoord is useful
- The need for CMCoord is constant
- CMCoord is inherently an interagency or "whole-of-government" responsibility in collaboration with NGOs and international bodies (so it "exercises" these increasingly important alliance "muscles" that can be valuable in a variety of regional contingencies)
- CMCoord is "exportable": it can help protect the homeland and third countries overseas, contributing to regional stability and multilateral security cooperation
- CMCoord is not politically controversial

The United States and Japan approach the CMCoord issue from different positions of strength and experience. The U.S. military is well funded and extremely capable, but it has been drawn into the disaster relief role in recent years at times reluctantly, given the combat and counter-insurgency demands it has faced since 2001. Japan's SDF [Self-Defense Forces] has a very high tempo of domestic relief operations, but it has relatively little experience overseas and limited projection capability. U.S. NGOs are better funded and have more international experience than their Japanese counterparts, but in Asia, Japan's NGOs often have complementary networks of local staff and technical expertise. Moreover, Japan's disaster relief teams can be a valuable asset.

A Core Crisis Group

Together with a handful of other key countries in Europe and East Asia, the United States and Japan can help form a valuable core crisis group that cooperates in support of large-scale, UN-led disaster relief operations. This kind of core group (of perhaps four to six nations) is generally more effective at making decisions and harmonizing policies and procedures than either a large collection of dozens of countries or uncoordinated efforts by individual countries, and it could provide invaluable support to the UN or to host nations in the early days following a disaster.

Maintaining CMCoord

Thinking about and taking steps to maintain CMCoord across the lifecycle of an event—from first response to last act of assistance—remains central to the concept of continuous operations that is so vital to a well-managed relief effort, since it is the military sprinters who buy the time that the civilian marathoners need to fully mobilize and eventually assume command in the recovery and reconstruction phase of an HA/DR [humanitarian assistance/disaster relief] operation.

It is probably too difficult (and unnecessary) to try to bridge the gaps between the military and civilian sectors for disaster relief situations in a comprehensive way. In other words, U.S.-Japan military-to-military interactions and parallel civilian-to-civilian interactions are likely to be much more productive than trying to integrate civil-military dialogues and policies across the alliance with any sort of regularity.

Japanese Forces Help in Haiti

Dispatched personnel: Total of 1,542 personnel (as of September [2011]).

An engineer unit has been working to help the recovery and reconstruction of Haiti since the great earthquake.

The United Nations Stabilization Mission in Haiti (MINUSTAH), which had been deployed in the country, decided to expand its military and police personnel to support the reconstruction after the earthquake. Upon the request of the United Nations, Japan dispatched an engineer unit of the JGSDF [Japan Ground Self-Defense Forces]. They cleared rubble, repaired roads, and constructed facilities, for example, and are continuing the activities in active cooperation with troops of other countries.

"The World Needs the Japan Self-Defense Forces," Japan Ministry of Defense, 2012.

A Master Key

Of course, these parallel civilian and military interactions need to be connected to each other in some way in order to set complementary goals and maintain communication and mutual awareness as they progress, but it is not necessary to impose common CMCoord solutions on the alliance. In this sense, American CMCoord and Japanese CMCoord will be like two different doors that open with their own key, but there should be a master key that can work both doors when the need arises. Developing this link between the two, in conjunction with the UN and other partners in the region, is a prime objective.

Overall, this linkage and these interactions should focus most on planning, preparation, communication, and assessment issues related to disaster relief, since actual operations are more likely to be carried out separately by U.S. and Japanese forces and civilian teams. Promoting joint U.S.-Japan disaster relief operations, therefore, should not be a specific goal of alliance managers, but more efficient and productive coordination of U.S. and Japanese contributions to these multinational operations is a worthwhile objective. This can start at the far end of the preparation and planning spectrum, including coordinated disaster reduction and capacity building through development assistance to disaster-prone countries, as well as adjusting (or perhaps adding to) prepositioned stockpiles of disaster relief supplies throughout the region.

Bilateral cooperation in this area can also move into more detailed planning tasks by identifying complementary specialties or a viable division of labor in certain circumstances, standardizing information flows (such as scripting requests for assistance and collaborating on advance contracting arrangements), and harmonizing damage- and needs-assessment procedures.

Theater Security Cooperation

Increasingly this kind of so-called theater security cooperation (TSC) involves more than just two allies working together, as shared interests in regional stability, open trade, anti-piracy and counterterrorism, disaster relief, and similar objectives are prompting more frequent collaboration amongst a wider variety of increasingly capable players. These joint exercises can include, it is worth noting, the construction of warehouses, supply depots, airstrips, and port facilities to which the allies might be granted access during future contingencies (as a part of "exercise-related construction").

The budgets supporting TSC and related training activities are relatively modest, however, and TSC is often perceived as competition for "real" needs. This kind of joint training, however, is an important part of training forces to conduct military operations in the challenging environment of coalition politics.

At the tactical and operational level, knowing how to work with forces from different cultural backgrounds and different doctrinal schools is critically important and difficult to learn from a book. The value of these training investments can be enhanced through more effective and timely coordination between the military and civilian officials and specialists.

Coordinating Countries' Resources

Another step in improving the ability of the United States and Japan to effectively pool their civilian and military resources in response to humanitarian crises is to identify and catalogue what assets (civil and military personnel, material and equipment, and support assets) are available to each country for HA/DR activities, particularly in Asia. This process should help familiarize U.S. and Japanese officials with one another's capacities to respond to a crisis, without necessarily committing either party to exchange logistics support and services. This exercise could also go beyond pinpointing available military assets, such as heavy-lift helicopters, naval vessels, and surveillance equipment, to reach into private-sector and NGO capabilities. Private-sector capabilities are particularly well suited to the areas of communication, damage assessment (involving commercial satellites and local NGO staff), and transportation.

Understanding the roles and resources of each actor involved in disaster relief creates familiarity at the strategic and operational levels of a mission, as well as helping to identify critical gaps in each country's disaster response capacities. In time, this process may lead to the development of a disaster management database, similar to OCHA's Central Register of Disaster Management Capacities. A bilateral inventory list specifying the civilian and military assets, support services, and personnel available for or, at minimum, trained for complex emergencies could enhance the capacity of the United States and Japan to respond, either alone or together, to an emerging crisis. Exchanging information on the availability of military assets would also help U.S. and Japanese planning efforts. But a bilateral effort in this area should be well coordinated with OCHA and other regional efforts, such as the contact points for the disaster relief database compiled by the ASEAN [Association of Southeast Asian Nations] Regional Forum (ARF). Databases such as these are notorious for becoming quickly outdated and inaccurate, and there is significant room to improve database development and management; this could be a productive area for enhancing efficiency through bilateral cooperation within multilateral frameworks.

Mutual Agreements Streamline Operations

Another means to improve government and military relations with NGOs and the private sector, as well as to enhance U.S.-Japan cooperation overall, is the establishment of mutual assistance and support agreements, or memorandums of understanding (MOUs), for disaster relief operations. The current U.S.-Japan Acquisition and Cross-Servicing Agreement enables U.S. and Japanese forces to provide mutual logistics support, exchange supplies—including food and fuel—and use each other's transportation and communications equipment, for reimbursement either in cash, replacement in kind, or equal value exchange. But the potential applicability of this agreement is not well understood in the broader disaster relief community, and although it can be used in disaster relief situations, it is not specifically designed to do so.

In addition to military-to-military MOUs, the two countries might study the benefits of signing MOUs with humanitarian and private-sector organizations. UN agencies, for example, have signed MOUs with several NGO and private-sector organizations, such as the International Federation of the Red Cross and Red Crescent Societies, OXFAM GB, and Deutsche Post World Net, the parent company of DHL, an international express and logistics company.

Standby Arrangements Enhance Mobilization

Standby arrangements for disaster management and emergency response between U.S. and Japanese civil and military partners would also enhance the ability of the two countries to mobilize resources quickly. A standby arrangement would commit each party to maintain specified resources on standby, such as technical and logistics resources, field staff, and material and equipment. Joint capacity-mapping exercises could help identify the allies' strengths and weaknesses, reveal which areas require additional investment, in terms of resources, personnel, and training, as well as determine which assets U.S. and Japanese forces should make available to one another to avoid duplications in assistance efforts. Moreover, this process could identify how best to integrate the UN, NGOs, and private-sector companies into disaster preparedness plans and relief efforts.

For now, standby arrangements for military capabilities might be difficult to implement, but introducing bilateral standby arrangements between U.S. and Japanese government agencies, NGOs, and private-sector companies is more feasible. OCHA [UN Office for the Coordination of Humanitarian Affairs] has had in place standby arrangements with governments and humanitarian organizations for the provision of emergency staff and equipment during disasters, and the UN Department of Peacekeeping has in place a similar arrangement, the UN Stand-by Arrangement System (UNSAS). Forums in East Asia have proposed establishing similar arrangements for regional disaster response and humanitarian activities, but the degree of U.S. and Japanese involvement in these programs has been limited, and neither is well aware of the other's national agreements, such as they are. The allies could compare and, when appropriate, further develop bilateral standby arrangements with relief agencies and commercial aircraft carriers and shipping companies, with an eye toward establishing an element of reciprocity with each other and perhaps with other nations and organizations.

Information Management

Information management is an overriding challenge for CMCoord, though this seemingly simple objective can mean slightly different things to different stakeholders. For many at OCHA, greater standardization of how information is provided by and managed among crisis response partners is the top priority for improving CMCoord. From their perspective, this includes information about the availability and capability of certain assets or personnel, the terms of their deployment, standardization of assessment reports and procedures, and a high degree of interoperability among the contributing organizations and governments.

For some this is a process of developing compatible systems, but others might emphasize training people to understand different responding organizations' capabilities and how they operate. Still others take this a step further and emphasize the personal relationships among responders in the field as the key factor. All of these perspectives are valid, but each of them suggests a slightly different focus for CMCoord training and cooperation in a bilateral (or mini-lateral) context. Developing practical options to increase and strengthen U.S.-Japan peer-to-peer interactions on CMCoord issues, while maintaining connections between these groups, should help the two countries to clarify how they can best contribute to the process of CMCoord improvement.

Strengthening the U.S.-Japan Alliance

Overall, strengthening the U.S.-Japan alliance for disaster response may increase the two countries' participation in regional and multilateral HA/DR missions, which will be a good thing for affected nations and for the alliance. Harmonizing policies and procedures among close allies would improve how they cooperate together or as members of a coalition, as well as pave the way for achieving a more efficient international framework for disaster response and recovery. Finally, opportunities for enhanced U.S.-Japan civil-military cooperation in disaster management and emergency response can serve as a catalyst for greater co-operation throughout the Asia-Pacific region for missions such as peacekeeping, counterproliferation, counterterrorism, and maritime security.

> "[The] mere presence [of the military] often endangers the relief and aid efforts, the local civilian population, aid workers and their own lives."

The Use of Military Forces for Disaster Relief Is Inappropriate and Harmful

Jamie Way

In the following viewpoint, the author views the emerging trend of utilizing military forces for disaster relief operations as troubling, pointing out that many perceive it to be imperialistic and even racist. She contends that the United States often justifies military intervention by citing human rights violations or the intention of protecting the population from terrorist or criminal violence. This trend is problematic, she maintains, because the military's expertise and top priority is security, not humanitarian aid. In the author's opinion, the military should not be used in humanitarian relief operations. Jamie Way is the research and communications coordinator of the Alliance for Global Justice.

As you read, consider the following questions:

1. According to a report in the *Telegraph*, cited by Way, how many US troops were on the ground in Haiti after the 2010 earthquake?
2. In what countries does Way report that human rights violations were used to justify US intervention?
3. Why does the author say that the United States was widely criticized for its occupation of Haiti's airport after the earthquake?

As the story of the tragedy in Haiti [the 2010 earthquake] continues to unfold, the spotlight seems to have turned away from the tragedy itself, and instead now largely focuses on the US military aid effort. Doctors Without Borders and the director of French aid have both complained that the U.S. military presence has impeded the progress of the relief mission. Many have noted that the priority of the military would appear to be security over rescue, causing the delivery of medical supplies to be postponed while the military brings its troops and supplies.

Both the UN and the US have increased troop levels. The *Telegraph* reports that the US has some 10,000 troops on the ground, and the UN is expected to add 3,000–9,000 more in addition to their force prior to the earthquake. This military response may be the result of a number of circumstances. Some claim that security problems and violence have been exaggerated. This could be due to historic racism and assumptions about Haitian culture. Others argue that military presence is benevolent and necessary for keeping the peace. And yet still, many have claimed that the increase of foreign military presence is an occupation and a continuation of US and foreign colonization and domination of the region.

Regardless of what troop increases may represent, they undoubtedly highlight a problematic trend in development aid effort: aid is often militarized.

Militarized Aid as Influence

Development aid has long been accused of being imperialistic, and with good reason. The concept of development aid truly came into fruition during the Cold War. Nervous about the temptations of communism for poor countries, and about maintaining hegemony in the developing world, the US developed the concept of foreign aid. In order to keep "poverty stricken" countries from falling prey to the USSR [Soviet Union], or from forging an independent political path, the US would seek to insure the continuation of its prized neoliberal economic system through the extension of aid to such countries.

Even beyond the state function of development, the most benevolent forms of its practice incorporated a distinctly Western set of assumptions about what made life valuable, and what made one "modern." Hoping to help the world achieve the level of comfort the West had attained, many idealists devoted their life to the goal of development. While for many these actions may have been good intentioned, they were (and often still are) Eurocentric. In the case of governmental programs, they have often been a political tool. Aid was offered as an incentive for policy changes within a country—policy changes dictated by Washington.

Aid As a Political Weapon

More recently, aid has developed into a multilateral instrument for enforcing neoliberal policies. This is evident in the requirements put forth by aid institutions such as the International Monetary Fund. Structural Adjustment Programs are enforced as a mechanism for implementing neoliberal policies in countries that accept international loans. Clearly, for many decades, the Global North [wealthy countries in the Northern Hemisphere] has employed the concept of aid and the promise of a life like "ours" as a way to incentivize certain behaviors and discourage others (be they cultural or economic). Development has been a tool for "winning hearts and minds" or at least twisting wrists until we can reach a compromise.

In the last decade, however, the use of aid as a political weapon has taken on even more dangerous and overtly hegemonic posture. The trend toward the militarization of aid has been met with great concern, but also, widespread acceptance. Suddenly, under this new paradigm, human rights are used to justify wars while help comes in the form of military presence. This trend is far from exclusive to Haiti, which up to this point may be amongst the mildest of such cases. Human rights violations were used to justify US intervention in Yugoslavia/Kosovo, Iraq and Afghanistan.

Militarized aid, and aid as a mechanism of counterterrorism, can be seen in countries such as Mali and Northern Uganda. Militaries have been sent to aid in disaster relief in New Orleans and Haiti. In an effort to galvanize popular support, US military efforts in Afghanistan have also begun to focus on providing aid. While these cases vary greatly in their justifications (disaster, drug trafficking, human rights violations, disasters, etc.), they all result in military presence as a function of delivering on the promises of humanitarian aid and protection of human rights.

Complicated Questions

Beyond the obvious questions that the militarization of aid raises about possible occupation, this phenomenon is problematic for a number of other reasons as well. It challenges the importance of expertise, priorities, dangers and risks, and the intent of providing aid.

If we learn nothing else from the Haiti example, it should now be obvious that the military's area of expertise is not humanitarian aid. Many argue that the military is able to mobilize faster and more efficiently than many other organizations and institutions. This is true, in the case of war. This is not necessarily the case with aid, however. The military consists of a highly trained group of individuals, but these individuals are not aid workers. They are primarily trained to kill and provide logistics for killing other

The U.S. Military Impedes Humanitarian Aid

The U.S. is using its position of power to impose its control over [Haiti] and impede relief efforts, turning away planes from Doctors Without Borders, the Mexican government and the Caribbean Community and Common Market. Jarry Emmanuel, the air logistics officer for the World Food Program, complained, "There are 200 flights going in and out every day, which is an incredible amount for a country like Haiti. But most of those flights are for the United States military. Their priorities are to secure the country." . . .

As anger among Haitians simmers over the lack of real relief, it is only a matter of time before heavily armed U.S. and UN forces open fire and kill innocent Haitians.

Ashley Smith, "Humanitarian Aid or Military Occupation?," Socialist Worker, January 19, 2010. http://socialistworker.org.

human beings. This training, even when there is a humanitarian component, does not develop the type of expertise necessary to be a good development practitioner. Regardless of how great the need and how well development workers knew the region, no one would ever suggest that they help fight a war, much less lead the battle. It is equally ridiculous to expect those trained in war and security issues to run a humanitarian relief effort.

Military Priorities Hinder Relief Efforts

Perhaps due to the fact that their training largely focuses on combat rather than relief efforts, the military tends to hold a distinct set of priorities. These priorities do not always bode well for relief missions. For example, the US has been widely criticized because during the critical 72 hours after the earthquake, the US military, which seized control of the airport, prioritized military flights over flights carrying medical supplies, doctors and relief experts. After a firestorm of international condemnation, they agreed, at least on paper, to give aid flights precedence. These actions were not simply due to lack of expertise in running a relief operation. The military sees its primary objective as creating and maintaining a secure atmosphere. Because their priority is security, rather than simply providing supplies, they often neglect supplying aid. Moreover, when aid is slow to arrive, it creates more desperate situations of violence and chaos.

The Issue of Neutrality

Another major issue that many aid organizations have taken with the militarization of aid is that it ruins their appearance of neutrality amongst warring populations. This critique, while based on the faulty assumption that an NGO [nongovernmental organization] can be neutral, does point to the increased danger that the militarization of aid has caused. In order to pursue a truly sustainable development, it is impossible to be apolitical. If relief aid and development are to be successful, it can only happen through a process of empowerment in which the marginalized confront the systems of power that have oppressed them. Political neutrality (in which power structures and systems of disenfranchisement are not challenged) is not a viable solution for organizations that wish to pursue a sustainable development that addresses the root causes of marginalization.

That being said, it is possible to avoid taking sides in particular conflicts. NGOs generally seek to remain neutral or uninvolved in local disagreements and official political disputes. But, when the military, often from the same country as the aid worker, arrives and plays the dual role of warrior and aid worker, NGO workers have difficulty distinguishing themselves and their political views from their armed countrymen. This jeopardizes not only the safety of the workers, but the success of the entire aid project.

The Role of Disaster Relief Aid

Aid, especially disaster relief aid, should not be used as a way to introduce economic policies, a way to exercise military might or a way to recruit supporters. Even if the aid supplied by militaries and governments were entirely altruistic, the simple fact remains that militaries are not aid experts. They do not have the same priorities that successful aid workers share. Their mere presence often endangers the relief and aid efforts, the local civilian population, aid workers and their own lives, by creating an atmosphere of fear and confusion. Aid should never (even appear to) be used as a weapon.

During great tragedies, many of us wish to lend a helping hand. But, despite the emergency atmosphere, we must be willing to take the time to look at the implications of our actions. In the case of Haiti, a history of violence, domination and paternalism is largely to blame for the almost unimaginable scope of the disaster. In this moment of need, we must not respond with more of the same. The global North's relief and aid efforts must not be shows of strength and power. Instead, they must simply assist Haiti as it determines its own future. As Haitians define their own rebirth, aid workers need to follow their lead, and the military needs to go home.

Periodical and Internet Sources Bibliography

The following articles have been chosen to supplement the diverse views presented in this chapter.

Donald McKinley Allen — "The Meaning of Big Government," Yahoo! Voices, August 28, 2011. http://voices.yahoo.com.

Joshua Hedland — "Why Is FEMA So Incompetent and Should It Be Abolished?," *PostLibertarian* (blog), August 27, 2011. www.postlibertarian.com.

Steve Kornacki — "When Republicans Suddenly Need Big Government," *Salon*, August 29, 2011. www.salon.com.

Matt Mayer — "Congress Should Act on FEMA's Refusal to Reform," Heritage Foundation, May 18, 2012. www.heritage.org.

Ryan Messmore — "Disaster Relief Shows Why Government Should Protect Good Samaritans," *Foundry* (blog), March 6, 2012. http://blog.heritage.org.

Dana Milbank — "Hurricane Irene and the Benefits of Big Government," *Washington Post*, August 29, 2011.

Napp Nazworth — "Disaster Relief: Does the Government Do Too Much?," *Christian Post*, August 28, 2011.

Jason Raznick — "Ron Paul Thinks FEMA Is the Real Disaster," *Forbes*, August 29, 2011.

Amanda Terkel — "FEMA Praised by Governors for Response to Hurricane Irene," *Huffington Post*, October 28, 2011. www.huffingtonpost.com.

Tyler Watts — "Disaster Response Restores Confidence in Government?," *Freeman*, January–February 2012.

OPPOSING
VIEWPOINTS®
SERIES

What Issues Surround the Media's Coverage of Natural Disasters?

Chapter Preface

In the past few decades, the rise of social media has revolutionized the way that most people communicate. Social media allows individuals to connect with many people at once and to share pictures, links to articles, and music. Users can receive updates on breaking news, services, and events. Videos can be uploaded to sites such as YouTube, Twitter, or Facebook and viewed by individuals around the world.

In recent years, social media have also assumed a key role during and after natural disasters by reporting information essential to disaster mitigation, recovery, and relief. National, state, and local governments have been able to utilize social media to communicate with citizens, first responders, other government officials, and the media. In fact, social media have become not only useful tools for law enforcement and emergency management services, but also for individuals communicating with family and friends during natural disasters.

The history of social networking can be traced back to 1971, when the first e-mail was sent. In 1978 Bulletin Board Systems (BBS) exchanged data over telephone lines with other users. Usenet, an early online bulletin board, utilized early web browsers. By 1995 Internet users were able to create their own websites, publish their own content, and interact with other people with similar interests. A few years later AOL introduced AOL Instant Messenger, which popularized the practice of instant messaging. Social networking sites such as SixDegrees.com allowed users to list family, friends, and other contacts and then post to a bulletin board and exchange messages with people on their list who were registered to the site.

In 2002 the popular social networking site Friendster was launched, registering more than 3 million users in its first three months. In the following decade, social networking technology and capability exploded: MySpace, Facebook, LinkedIn, Mixi,

Skype, Twitter, and a number of other social networking sites thrived in a competitive environment. These sites were created for online socializing and fun.

However, social media became vital tools during and after natural disasters, too. After Japan's massive earthquake and tsunami in 2011, relief organizations immediately took to Twitter to post information about tsunami alerts, shelter locations for the displaced and homeless, and disaster recovery operations. Survivors were able to communicate with family and friends all over the world. Charities were able to mobilize aid and solicit donations from the public quickly.

Later that same year, an earthquake struck Virginia and traveled up the East Coast. Almost immediately people in the region took to Twitter, Facebook, and other social networking sites to find out what had happened and post their personal stories. News of the earthquake appeared on social networking sites before it was reported on TV news or on the radio. According to Facebook, the word "earthquake" appeared in the status updates of 3 million users within four minutes of the quake. On Twitter, users were sending out fifty-five hundred tweets per second—making it one of the busiest times ever recorded on the site.

Although social media sites were established for online socializing, they have become increasingly essential for responding to all types of crises all over the world. Governments and humanitarian groups recognize the value of social networking in disaster response and relief efforts and are working to find ways to create and exploit flexible, immediate, and accessible video and text channels of communication to better provide essential services.

Experts believe that social media will have an increasingly essential role in reporting events and sharing information during and after natural disasters. The role of more-traditional broadcast media is explored in the following chapter, which discusses the quality of media coverage, the effect of graphic video footage and photos on viewers and readers, and the issues surrounding the performance of physician reporters.

> *"The reporting of cataclysms or lesser disasters is often wildly misleading."*

Reporting on Natural Disasters Is Often Superficial and Misleading

Patrick Cockburn

In the following viewpoint, a writer maintains that media coverage of natural disasters is not an accurate reflection of what happens but, rather, a misleading version of reality colored by stereotyping, bias, superficial and formulaic reporting, and an instinct to exaggerate and dramatize events. He argues that disaster reporting is difficult to do and often repetitious and dull. Because a reporter feels pressured to feign an emotional response to the devastation and human suffering, he contends, media coverage can seem tired and contrived; moreover, he adds, media coverage of natural disasters is short-lived, as interest fades when nothing new and exciting happens. Patrick Cockburn is an author and prize-winning journalist.

As you read, consider the following questions:

1. How many people does Cockburn report died in the 2010 earthquake in Haiti?

2. According to the author, to what did *New York Times* journalist Paul Krugman compare New York mayor Michael Bloomberg's response to a recent blizzard?
3. In what year does Cockburn say that the story of the Islamic charities emerged?

The media generally assume that news of war, crime and natural disasters will always win an audience. "If it bleeds, it leads," is a well-tried adage of American journalism. Of the three categories, coverage of war has attracted criticism for its lies, jingoism and general bias. Crime reporting traditionally exaggerates the danger of violence in society, creating an unnecessary sense of insecurity.

The Nature of Disaster Reporting

Media coverage of natural disasters—floods, blizzards, hurricanes, earthquakes and volcanoes—is, on the contrary, largely accepted as an accurate reflection of what really happened. But in my experience, the opposite is true: the reporting of cataclysms or lesser disasters is often wildly misleading. Stereotyping is common: whichever the country involved, there are similar images of wrecked bridges, half-submerged houses and last-minute rescues.

The scale of the disaster is difficult to assess from news coverage: are we seeing or reading about the worst examples of devastation, or are these the norm? Are victims in the hundreds or the millions? Most usually the extent of the damage and the number of casualties are exaggerated, particularly in the developed world. I remember covering floods on the Mississippi in the 1990s and watching as a wall of cameras and cameramen focused on a well-built house in a St Louis suburb which was slowly disappearing under the water. But just a few hundred yards away, ignored by all the cameramen, a long line of gamblers was walking unconcernedly along wooden walkways to board a river boat casino.

The reporting of natural disasters appears easy, but it is difficult to do convincingly. Over the past year, a series of calamities or, at the least, surprisingly severe weather, has dominated the news for weeks at a time. Just over a year ago, Haiti had its worst earthquake in 200 years, which killed more than 250,000 people. In August [2011], exceptionally heavy monsoon rains turned the Indus river into a vast dangerous lake, forcing millions of Pakistani farmers to flee their homes and take refuge on the embankments. Less devastating was unexpectedly heavy snow in Britain in December and the severe blizzard which struck New York at Christmas. In the first half of January, the news was once again being led by climatic disasters: the floods in Queensland and the mudslides in Brazil.

The Novelty Has Worn Off

All these events are dramatic and should be interesting, but the reporting of them is frequently repetitious and dull. This may be partly because news coverage of all disasters, actual or forecast, is delivered in similarly apocalyptic tones. Particularly in the US, weather dramas are so frequently predicted that dire warnings have long lost their impact. This helps to explain why so many people are caught by surprise when there is a real catastrophe, such as Hurricane Katrina breaking the levees protecting New Orleans in 2005 and flooding the city. US television news never admits the role it plays in ensuring that nobody takes warnings of floods and hurricanes too seriously because they have heard it all before.

Governments are warier than they used to be in dealing with disasters, conscious of the political damage they will suffer if they are seen as unfeeling or unresponsive to climatic emergencies. The best-remembered single picture of the New Orleans flood is probably not of water rushing through the streets, but of President Bush peering at it with distant interest out of the window of his aircraft from several thousand feet above the devastation.

Disaster Reporting in the UK

UK natural disasters are, thanks to the mild climate, not really in the same league as other countries'. Flooding in the Lake District hardly compares with what happened in Brisbane [Australia]. The same broken or unsafe bridges are filmed again and again. The tone of the reporting is always doleful and, at times, funereal. Worst cases are presented as typical. The pre-Christmas snow and consequent transport difficulties were spoken of as if everybody in Britain spent their entire time longing to get to work instead of welcoming an excuse to stay at home. The simple pleasure of not having to do anything is underplayed and there is never a mention of the fact that the cities and countryside of Britain are at their most beautiful when they are under a blanket of snow.

There is a further difficulty in reporting British disasters, particularly for television and radio. The British still seem, despite some evidence to the contrary—such as in the aftermath of the death of Diana, Princess of Wales—to be genuinely stoical and emotionally tough. It is touching to see reporters baffled and irritated by the refusal of British flood victims, whose living rooms are knee-deep in sewage and water, to treat what has happened to them as more than an unlucky mishap which is not going to ruin their lives.

This British stoicism appears to be quite real even under the most intense pressure. I was in Baghdad in 1990 when British hostages who had been passengers on a British Airways flight that had landed in Kuwait were released just as the Iraqi army was invading. They had then been taken to military camps, power stations, refineries and other Iraqi facilities to deter the US and UK from bombing them. In December that year, [Iraqi dictator] Saddam Hussein decided to release his prisoners as a propaganda gesture, the first being freed in front of us journalists in the Al-Rashid hotel in Baghdad. To the frustration of television correspondents and photographers, almost all the former hostages refused to blub to order and seemed impressively unmarked and lacking in self-pity after their ordeal. Television cameras clustered around a single man, evidently drunk, who spoke brokenly of his grim experiences.

Pampered Journalists

Some of the most passionate writing about recent extreme weather episodes in New York and London come not from those who were badly hit but from columnists possibly unaccustomed to inconvenience and discomfort. Philip Stephens wrote an eloquent and bitter piece in the *Financial Times* about the misery of having, after a long flight, to wait an extra three hours in his aircraft at Heathrow because there was nowhere for it to dock. Paul Krugman of the *New York Times* compared the failure of New York's Mayor, Michael Bloomberg, to cope with the blizzard with that of President Bush after Hurricane Katrina. Reminded that some 1,500 people had died in the hurricane and casualties in New York were minimal, he later withdrew the comparison with some embarrassment.

Popular response to natural disasters is scarcely an accurate guide to national characteristics. Other factors may come into play in promoting stoicism and endurance, notably the possession of an insurance policy covering possible damage. After Hurricane Andrew struck south of Miami in 1992, I remember seeing people squatting in the ruins of their wooden houses with large notices telling passing insurance adjusters that the ruined house was still inhabited and they wanted to see him or her. Not surprisingly they were a lot more philosophical about their plight than Haitians in Port-au-Prince or farmers in the Punjab [province of Pakistan].

Stories Fade from Headlines

Once the initial drama of a disaster is over, coverage frequently dribbles away because nothing new is happening. I remember how bizarre the foreign editor of the newspaper I was then working for found it that I should want to go back to Florida a month after Hurricane Andrew to see what had happened to the victims. "I am not sure that is still a story," he responded sourly to what he evidently considered a highly eccentric request.

I could see his point. After a day or two, accounts of disasters sound very much the same. There are the same bemused refugees on the road or in a camp of tents or huts; houses destroyed by an earthquake, be it in Kashmir or Haiti, look like squashed concrete sandwiches; the force of the water in rivers in flood often leaves nothing standing but a few walls and some rubble. Every disaster has uplifting rescue stories when a few survivors are miraculously pulled alive from the wreckage of houses. Refugees always complain, often with reason, about the slow response of their government and the aid agencies.

Even a little looting is reported as a general breakdown of law and order. Post–the Iraq war, most media companies or their insurance companies have contracts with security companies which have every incentive to emphasise the threat to journalists. In Haiti, where the danger was minimal, many correspondents were wearing body armour as if they were on the road out of Kabul [Afghanistan].

I have always had sympathy for looters, who are usually just very poor people with every reason to hate the powers that be. I was once in a police station in Haiti that was being systematically torn apart, with looters carefully extracting nails from the woodwork for later sale in the market. They were so good at their work that the stairs collapsed, marooning other looters on the first storey of the police station. I always found in Iraq that the presence or absence of looters is a useful pointer as to how risky a situation really is, since only extreme danger will deter the thieves.

Limited Life of Disaster Stories

Even the worst of disasters has a limited life as a news story unless something new happens. The Indus floods which started last July [2010] were like any great flood, except that their extent was enormous and the waters very slow to subside. In this vacuum of fresh news, spurious reports took life. One claimed that Islamic fundamentalist charities were taking advantage of the failure of the government and Western air agencies to act and were spreading Islamic militancy among angry and receptive refugees. Journalists liked this story because they know that the suggestion that "Islamic fundamentalist militants" are at work will revive the most dead-in-the-water story in the eyes of a news editor. Islamic militants also promote the tale, and are happy to confirm it, because it shows them as more influential and active than they in fact are.

The story of the Islamic militant charities first emerged during the Kashmir earthquake of 2005 and was widely believed. Eventually, the World Bank, which found that donors were discouraged by the idea that aid was falling into the hands of militants, felt compelled to fund a survey of Kashmiri villagers to disprove the story.

I have always found that the most interesting part of reporting disasters, which brings them to life in my mind, is the way in which they reveal, like nothing else, what a society is really like. I had often been in Miami before Hurricane Andrew struck, but until it was destroyed by the wind and I went to see it, I never realised that there was a sprawling town, its one-storey houses largely made out of wood, to the south of Miami, where workers in the city and in the fruit plantations had their homes. It was not the sort of place that ever appeared in *Miami Vice* or *CSI: Miami.*

Last September, I was in Rajanpur in south Punjab looking at the havoc caused by the Indus floods. I asked how many people had died in one area and was told, as if this was to be expected, that a number of those who had died had been hostages held in their heavily fortified headquarters in the flood plain by local bandits who had manacled them. They had not had time to free them from their chains as the waters of the Indus rose and they had all drowned. It had never occurred to me before, as in Iraq and parts of Afghanistan, that the Punjab had its quota of professional kidnappers and bandits too powerful for the police to deal with.

A central reason why the reporting of natural disasters so often sounds contrived and formulaic is that the journalist feels that he or she must pretend to [have] an emotional response on their own part and that of their audience, which is not really there. It is one thing to feel grief for a single person or a small group whom one knows, but very difficult to feel the same way over the death or misery of thousands one has never met.

I was in Belfast [Northern Ireland] in 1974 at the height of the bombings and sectarian killings. I remember saying to a friend, an MP [Member of Parliament] called Paddy Devlin, that I was shocked by some particularly nasty bomb attack that had killed or mutilated a dozen people. He derided my reaction as spurious. "You don't really feel that," he said. "Nobody who lives here with so many people being shot or blown apart every day can have an emotional reaction to every death. The truth is we don't really feel anything unless something happens to a member of our family or the half-dozen people we are closest to."

> "The impact of [natural-disaster reporting] is that we become desensitised to the magnitude and human tragedy of these disasters."

Formulaic Natural-Disaster Reporting Undermines Aid Efforts and Stereotypes Victims

Simon Moss

In the following viewpoint, the author points out that media coverage of natural disasters follows a general formula, as evinced by reporting on the 2010 Haitian earthquake and the Pakistan floods. He argues that there are three negative consequences of this pattern: aid efforts are always portrayed as too slow or ineffective; people are depicted as either victims or criminals; and local disaster relief efforts are rarely shown. As a result, he says, viewers become desensitized to the human tragedy and victims become stereotypes. If individuals want to help, the author concludes, they should contribute to organizations that focus on disaster preparedness. Simon Moss is the cofounder and chief operating officer of the Global Poverty Project.

Simon Moss, "Reporting on Natural Disasters in Poor Countries," Global Poverty Project online, December 30, 2010. GlobalPovertyProject.com. Copyright © 2010 by Global Poverty Project. All rights reserved. Reproduced by permission.

As you read, consider the following questions:

1. What are the four different stories that Moss says the media report about poor countries?
2. What happens on day 6 of Moss's hypothetical report from Equatorial Kundu?
3. When does Moss believe that there will be notable spikes in reporting after a natural disaster?

I'll admit it, I'm a news junkie. Ten or so times a day I'll check the news headlines, looking for anything new that's relevant to me. As someone whose job it is to communicate extreme poverty, that means looking out for any news from the world's poorest countries (or as the media tend to call it, "Africa" or "Asia").

After several years doing this, I've discovered that the media have four different stories that they file on poor countries—corruption, conflict, crazy and catastrophe. Each hook has its merits and drawbacks, but recently, stories about large-scale natural disasters have started to follow a rather unhelpful pattern, which goes something like this:

The Pattern

Day 1: We have reports of a massive disaster in Equatorial Kundu (cue graphic showing location of country on a map). Hundreds, thousands or maybe even tens of thousands of (coloured) people are feared dead. We also have unconfirmed reports that several of our (white) citizens may have been involved.

Day 2: It's a lot worse than we thought. The government of Equatorial Kundu have urgently asked for help from the international community. The Prime Minister said today that we stand in solidarity with the people of Equatorial Kundu, and will provide all possible assistance. Oxfam and other aid agencies have launched an appeal for the victims of this disaster, which you can give to on this number. The death toll is expected to climb dramatically in the coming days, and we can now confirm that at least one of our own nationals has died.

Day 3: We can take you now via a phone link to our journalist, who has just landed in Equatorial Kundu . . .

It's a scene of total devastation here, I've never seen anything like it. The local government has been overwhelmed, and as aid agencies arrive, the local people are desperate for help. As I picked through the ruins, I met people who had lost their whole families.

Day 4: Our reporter on the ground in Equatorial Kundu reports:

A day after I arrive, I'm shocked at the magnitude of this disaster. But, amidst the tragedy, there are amazing stories of hope, people being pulled from the rubble by family members who had searched for days.

I'm here with a representative from an aid agency.

(pan to aid worker)

The people of Equatorial Kundu urgently need your help. We have launched an appeal to provide for urgently needed food, water and shelter for these people. It will take months, years . . . (cut off by journalist)

Thanks, back to you in the studio.

Day 5: Tonight we take you live to Equatorial Kundu, where serious questions are being asked about aid efforts:

Five days after this country was changed forever, aid is nowhere to be seen. The first supplies have arrived, but aid agencies have failed to reach people on the ground.

Day 6: Miracle survival stories:

Almost a week after the disaster, and amidst ongoing claims that aid agencies are failing to respond, tonight we bring you a story of hope. In the last 24 hours, we've seen people pulled from the rubble, still alive.

(cut to dramatic rescue footage, emotional relatives crying in relief)

Day 7:

Aid has finally started to reach victims of the Kundu disaster, but there are increasing concerns about disease and civil disorder. Tens of thousands of people made homeless by the disaster are tonight sheltering under tents provided by relief efforts. A huge logistical effort is under way to provide food, water and shelter for them. But, as bodies continue to rot under the rubble, health experts fear a major outbreak of cholera. And, there are reports of civil disorder as people overwhelm the meagre aid supplies, and gangs loot deserted shops.

Then, the disaster starts to fall away from the headlines for a few days, there being no miracles to report. Until, suddenly . . .

Around day 10: Tonight we bring you a special report from the countryside of Equatorial Kundu:

Here, a few hours outside of the capital, it's like the disaster struck yesterday. 10 days after the world's attention was so tragically focused on this country, I can report the shocking fact that aid efforts have completely failed to reach this community. Despite the huge sums of money raised for relief efforts, locals tell me that they've received no aid. For them, it's too little, too late.

The Next Phase

Stories will appear with decreasing frequency in the following weeks, with notable spikes at the one-, three- and six-month marks. All of these stories will be punctuated by the theme, "very little has changed here. Thousands still live in emergency tents and disease remains a daily threat. Aid agencies say the recovery will take longer, but the international community

The Media and Stereotypes

A stereotype is an oversimplification of groups of people. This oversimplification is a cognitive process that involves beliefs about and expectations of these groups. Stereotypes reinforce the status quo, and restrict diversity of social roles that individuals may hold. Complex information, such as characteristics of diverse groups, is understood and remembered by people who draw upon abstracted knowledge, often unconsciously, based on experience—real or vicarious. Many people use media experiences to organize their thoughts about a concept. Media draw on recognizable stereotypes both as a matter of convenience and in order to convey a point.

Manoucheka Celeste, "Reporting Natural Disasters," Dart Center for Journalism and Trauma, January 9, 2011.

is growing impatient that aid efforts have been slow and piecemeal."

This is the narrative that played out twice this year, with examples of coverage from the BBC for the Haiti earthquake or the Pakistan floods. Along with the fictional example above, these show how a series of factually correct stories add up to a narrative with three negative consequences.

Aid efforts are always portrayed as too slow/ineffective. Delivering aid in disaster areas is hard. Even though much of the criticism levelled at aid efforts during disasters is warranted, doing this through the media means that the public are bombarded with inconsistent messages. On the one hand, we're being urged to give, yet at the same time, we're being told that our donations aren't making a difference, and that aid organisations are incompetent. The result—rising levels of public concern about aid effectiveness, and the belief that aid doesn't work.

People in disaster are only ever shown as victims or criminals. Given how seldom we actually encounter people in poor countries, we tend to generalise from the images that we see in the media. The consequence of media coverage of disasters is that we implicitly feel that all people in poor countries must be like the victims or criminals that we see in reports. That frames our broader response to people in poverty, reinforcing the idea that we need to "save" these people—from disasters and themselves.

Related to this, coverage of disasters almost never mentions local efforts to respond. Local charities, local government and local people are nowhere to be seen. The history, politics, economy, geography and culture of a country becomes irrelevant as it's reduced to an icon of suffering. By missing the good and bad of a country, the message becomes one of us (rich, white, western) needing to go in and "fix" these countries.

The impact of all of this is that we become desensitised to the magnitude and human tragedy of these disasters. We come to see them as just part of a broader narrative of hopelessness and incompetence in "Africa" and "Asia," and we're left with the impression that there's nothing we can do to help.

But, there's much that we can do to help. It starts with supporting organisations who work on disaster preparedness, so communities are better able to manage if things do go wrong. It's about supporting broader efforts to enable good governance and fight corruption, so that if disasters do happen, the local government is trusted and equipped to respond. And, it's about taking the news with a rather large grain of salt.

> *"Like any X-rated content, this smut [disaster reporting] is all flesh and no substantive plot."*

Sensationalist Disaster Coverage Ignores Important Economic and Political Issues

David Sirota

In the following viewpoint, the author characterizes media coverage of the 2010 earthquake in Haiti and its aftermath as "disaster porn"—more focused on sensationalizing the tragedy than providing basic information on how Haiti had become so poor and ill-equipped to deal with such a major disaster to begin with. He argues that some historical background and economic and political context into the situation in Haiti was essential to understand the country's reaction to the catastrophe and its unique challenges in rebuilding and moving forward. Instead, he contends, we were faced with a media that attempted to avoid "politicization" of the crisis and provided superficial, misleading, and exploitative coverage. David Sirota is a blogger, author, and syndicated columnist.

As you read, consider the following questions:

1. What is the unemployment rate in Haiti, according to Sirota?

2. What does the author say destroyed Haiti's agricultural economy in the 1990s?

3. What does Sirota believe that the media show instead of providing essential historical background on what made Haiti so poor?

The black t-shirt—so tight, so come-hither. And oh, those safari button-downs—joke-worthy on Eddie Bauer mannequins, but on news correspondents, so . . . enticing.

America missed these sartorial seductions, pined for their sweet suggestive nothings. And now, finally, a nation of television addicts can thank its disaster pornographers for bringing back the lurid garments—and the lustful voyeurism they evoke.

Yes, thousands of miles from the San Fernando Valley's seedy [porn] studios, the adult entertainment business is alive and panting in Haiti. This year's luminaries aren't the industry's typical muscle-bound mustaches of machismo—they are NBC's Brian Williams pillow-talking to the camera in his Indiana Jones garb, CNN's Sanjay Gupta playing doctor and, of course, CNN's Anderson Cooper in that two-sizes-too-small t-shirt "rarely missing an opportunity to showcase his buff physique," as the *New York Times* gushed. They are all the disaster porn stars in the media with visions of Peabodys and Pulitzers dancing in their heads.

And We the Ogling People drink it in.

Where Is the Historical Context?

Like any X-rated content, this smut is all flesh and no substantive plot. The lens flits between body parts and journalists pulling perverse [iconic news anchor Walter] Cronkite-in-Vietnam impressions (at one point, CNN showed Cooper and his t-shirt saving a child). But there is little discussion of how western Hispaniola [the island that Haiti makes up half of] was a manmade disaster before an earthquake made it a natural one.

Though neighboring the planet's wealthiest nation, Haiti has long been one of the world's poorest places. It sports 80 percent

> ## Titillating with Disaster Porn
>
> This horror-porn hints at a serious crisis of values in modern journalism. Many hacks now appear more interested in describing their own reactions to events than uncovering the facts about those events, and objective reporting is increasingly being replaced by a sub-Dante search for signs of hell, depravity and indignity.
>
> *Brendan O'Neill, "Haiti Earthquake*
> *Reporters Titillate with Disaster Porn," The*
> *Week, January 19, 2010.*
> *www.theweek.com.*

unemployment and a GDP [gross domestic product] smaller than the annual executive bonus fund at a single Wall Street bank. The destitution is tragic—and a reflection, in part, of colonial domination.

For much of the last two centuries, Western powers used embargo threats to force the country's population of erstwhile slaves to reimburse their former European masters for lost "property." As Harvard's Henry Louis Gates recounts, America aided these efforts from the beginning because President Thomas Jefferson feared a successful black republic would "inspire slave insurrections throughout the American South."

Crushed by this oppression, Haiti was then assaulted in the 1990s by American "free" trade policies that destroyed its agricultural economy and tried to turn the country into the world's sweatshop.

In recent years, as the menace of Western-backed coups lurked, Haiti has at times been compelled to pay more interest on its debt than it received in foreign aid.

The Real Story of Haiti

This is the real story of Haiti that the black t-shirts and safari button-downs (and, alas, their viewers) have never cared about. They've only noticed the country when a cataclysm provided more telegenic images than the daily death and despair of the island's pre-earthquake squalor.

Even now, as the casualty count rises, disaster pornographers barely mention the macabre history. They know that doing so would break unspoken rules against holding up a foreign policy mirror to America and against riling the politicians and business interests that contributed to Haiti's demise.

Rather than reporting on what made Haiti so poor and therefore its infrastructure so susceptible to collapse, we get clips of Haitians momentarily cheering "USA!" as food packages trickle into their devastated capital. Rather than inquiries about how poverty made Haiti so ill-prepared for rescue operations, the disaster pornographers instead obediently follow [US president] George W. Bush, who self-servingly says, "You've got to deal with the desperation and there ought to be no politicization of that."

"Politicization"—so that's the safe-for-TV euphemism they're using these days, huh? Evidently, it must be avoided—evidently, nothing kills an audience's heaving passion faster than "politics" or (God forbid) contextualized news.

Anything like that—anything beyond the exploitation of raw disaster porn—well, it might ruin the money shot.

> "It's time we stopped speaking of 'porn'
> in relation to photographic portrayals
> [of disasters]."

Startling Disaster Imagery Encourages Empathy and Increases Assistance for Victims

David Campbell

In the following viewpoint, the author suggests that the trend of classifying visual representations of the suffering of others as "disaster pornography" should be rejected because it shows an aesthetic or moral judgment and dismisses concerns about a lack of empathy for disaster victims with one easy slogan. He contends that using "pornography" is just a lazy substitute for the painful self-examination it would take to determine why there seems to be a failure of empathy for natural disaster victims. Although there needs to be a lot more analysis of the problem to get to the true issue, he concludes, abandoning the use of the term "disaster porn" is a step forward. David Campbell is a writer, editor, and producer.

As you read, consider the following questions:
1. According to Campbell, when did the idea emerge that sympathy for others is one of the characteristics of a modern, feeling individual?
2. What does the author argue about compassion fatigue?
3. What does Campbell believe that photographs of suffering are a threat to?

"Development pornography". "Poverty porn". "Disaster porn". "Ruin porn". "War porn". "Famine porn". "Stereotype porn". When it comes to the representation of atrocity and suffering, the charge of pornography abounds.

What does it mean to use this term so frequently in relation to so many different situations? What are the conditions supposedly signified by "pornography"? Might this singular term obscure more than it reveals?

Disaster Porn

With last week's anniversary of Haiti's 2010 earthquake I recalled a BBC Radio 4 segment that asked if the news photographs of the disaster were too graphic. John Humphreys introduced the segment as follows:

> Disaster pornography. It's a powerful and disturbing phrase, coined by Brendan Gormley, the man who runs the Disasters and Emergencies Committee, to describe what so often emerges after a terrible tragedy like Haiti. You know exactly what he means—the pictures of victims that show in shocking detail what's happened to them, stripped of life and often stripped of dignity.

Humphreys was wrong on the origin of the term because it predates Gormley's usage by a long way. In NGO [nongovernmental organization] circles it has been common for some time, and, as I shall argue below, it has a very long conceptual history.

But Humphreys's statement—"You know exactly what he means"—is revealing. "Pornography", he suggests, is a term that invokes a conventional wisdom, something we know without having to be told, something we can identify without even looking.

What It Means to Be Pornographic

Like all concepts that seem natural it needs unpacking. To consider what the frequent use of "pornography" to describe the representation of suffering involves I want to draw on the historian Carolyn Dean's research to suggest it's time we stopped speaking of "porn" in relation to photographic portrayals.

Let me be clear on two points, though. The first is that there are representations or objects that can be analysed as pornographic, so dispensing with the concept in relation to picturing atrocity is not to argue it is inapplicable in all other circumstances. The second is that the problems and limitations in photography sometimes identified via the label of "pornography" are serious and in need of remedy. The reliance on stereotypes, among many other problems, has to be addressed. It's just that labelling these concerns "pornography" doesn't get us far.

So why has "porn" become a common term of critique, and what are its limitations?

Some Historical Perspective

From the eighteenth century onwards, during the Enlightenment, sympathy for others was deemed to be one of the characteristics of a modern, feeling individual. This was part of a general cultural change that gave rise to humanitarianism—compassion and a reluctance to inflict pain were marked as civilized values with cruelty deemed barbaric and savage.

With development reducing the daily experience of suffering, people were motivated to help others through representations that offered symbolic proximity to the victim. From the beginning, long before the technology of photography, there were cultural worries about perceived impediments to empathy, such as images and narratives that produced insufficient compassion or disingenuous sympathy.

The recent history of "pornography" as a term for cultural anxiety demonstrates how it names many things but explains few. The modern concept of "pornographic" emerged in the 1880s when, Dean argues, authorities in America and Europe sought to control literature that "provoked antisocial sexual sensations and acts in those deemed morally weak or unformed—women, children and working-class men." They feared that the goal of a "normal," healthy population would be undermined by the expression of inappropriate desires.

After World War One, in addition to sexually explicit material, the idea of "pornography" migrated to representations of suffering that allegedly dehumanized and objectified their subjects, usually veterans. World War Two saw this usage intensify with, for example, James Agee (the writer who worked with Walker Evans on *Let Us Now Praise Famous Men*) declaring that the newsreel footage from the battle at Iwo Jima was degrading to anyone who looked at it because it created an "incurable distance" between the subject and viewer.

From 1960 onwards this sense of "porn" as a barrier to identification with victims was accelerated by discussions around the representation of the Holocaust, and Dean spends much of *The Fragility of Empathy* dealing with the numerous examples where the charge of "pornography" dominates debate about which visual representations of the Nazi genocide were permissible.

Treats to Empathy

In the evaluation of ourselves as human and civilised, "we" have often expressed anxieties about our collective ability to feel compassion. What Dean calls "threats to empathic identification" have been repeatedly identified since the eighteenth century, and today "bad images" are high on the suspect list. In this context our cultural anxieties are expressed via another of those oft-repeated slogans that pretend to offer an explanation—"compassion fatigue." As Dean writes:

> Assertions that we are numb and indifferent to suffering, that exposure to narratives and images of suffering has generated new and dramatic forms of emotional distance, however they are transmitted, are by now commonplace in both the United States and western Europe.

In photographic circles, this view is another conventional wisdom. For example, in his review of the 2010 *Exposed* exhibition at the Tate [Gallery in London], Gerry Badger wrote that he found the show, despite its sections dealing with sexual voyeurism and violence, a little "tame":

> I don't think this sense of tameness was simply a result of critics' déjà vu, but something more fundamental. I think it may also reflect Susan Sontag's point, made in her book *On Photography* (1977)—an extremely prescient point in pre-internet days. Writing about the effect of increased exposure to pornographic or violent photographs, she remarked: "Once one has seen such images, one has started down the road of seeing more—and more. Images transfix. Images anaesthetise."
>
> This brings us to a crucial issue. Sontag's "road" has become a 12-lane superhighway. It's the issue—perhaps largely unseen, but certainly not unspoken—that hangs over *Exposed*, just outside the galleries, like the seven-eighths of an iceberg that lies underwater—the ubiquity, and incredible proliferation of photographic images in our society thanks (if that is the right word) to the Internet. Not just in terms of numbers, but in terms of the almost total lack of control regarding their content.

Badger's statement expresses the anxieties perfectly—the proliferation of images, the lack of control over their content, and the inevitable dulling of our moral senses. No matter how neat the associations between images and action (or lack thereof), and no matter how often it is repeated, we can't get away from the fact that this is just a claim unsupported by evidence. Indeed, I argue that compassion fatigue is a myth.

There is, of course, much more work to be done detailing the evidence to support my position, but I made some preliminary remarks to this effect at the LCC's [London College of Communication's] "Third Image" symposium in December 2009. . . . However, there is one indisputable counterpoint to Badger we can easily note: his *de rigeur* reference to the early Sontag overlooks the fact the argument was reversed in her final book, *Regarding the Pain of Others* (2003), where she stated such claims about the failure of atrocity images had become a cliché. Sontag's road, even as a superhighway, doesn't go in the direction Badger and so many others describe.

All That "Porn" Signifies

I've noted above the complex history of "pornography" and its varied use in different contexts. Dean calls "porn" a promiscuous term, and when we consider the wide range of conditions it attaches itself to, this pun is more than justified. As a signifier of responses to bodily suffering, "pornography" has come to mean the violation of dignity, cultural degradation, taking things out of context, exploitation, objectification, putting misery and horror on display, the encouragement of voyeurism, the construction of desire, unacceptable sexuality, moral and political perversion, and a fair number more.

Furthermore, this litany of possible conditions named by "pornography" is replete with contradictory relations between the elements. Excesses mark some of the conditions while others involve shortages. Critics, Dean argues, are also confused about whether "pornography" is the cause or effect of these conditions.

The upshot is that a term with a complex history, a licentious character and an uncertain mode of operation fails to offer an argument or a framework for understanding the work images do. It is at one and the same time too broad and too empty, applied to so much yet explaining so little. As a result, Dean concludes that "pornography"

> functions primarily as an aesthetic or moral judgement that *precludes* an investigation of traumatic response and arguably *diverts* us from the more explicitly posed question: how to forge a critical use of empathy? (emphasis added)

I think this is correct. The repeated and indiscriminate use of "porn" is a substitute for evidence in arguments about the alleged exhaustion of empathy. "Porn" has become part of a fable that asserts we fail to recognise our ethical obligations towards others, and have become habituated to suffering because so many pictures have become threats to empathic identification.

The Issues That Remain

Long on assertion and short on evidence, "pornography" should be dispensed with as a term related to visual representations of suffering. However, that is *not* the same as arguing that all is right with conventional photographs of atrocity and disaster. Many of the problems "porn" attached itself to must be dealt with in relation to specific images in specific contexts, and many of the previous posts here [on my blog] have attempted to do that. It is just that aggregating those concerns under one banner prevents us from engaging the problems properly.

We also need to ask some hard questions about what and where are the main threats to empathy. In the wake of two world wars and a century of genocide, our inability to stop the suffering of others has been painfully demonstrated. Our collective failure produces cultural anxieties, and they have been exacerbated by our post-WWII condition. Simultaneously we have developed a greater awareness of distant atrocities because of media technologies, and a human rights culture that details responsibilities with regard to people beyond our immediate borders. "Pornography" and "compassion fatigue" are alibis, slogans that substitute for answers to this gap between heightened awareness and limited response, which is limited at least in relation to the scale of the challenges.

Has there been a failure of empathy in recent times? I'm not sure. The size and vitality of the charity sector, whatever the problems with NGOs, might be evidence of on-going ethical commitments. Are photographs of suffering a threat to empathy? Some are, and some are not, but we need to know a lot more about how people actually respond to images before we can offer definitive conclusions. What if, rather than being emotionally exhausted, any lack of empathy comes from people deciding they just don't want to know about atrocity regardless of the nature of the available pictures? There is much more thought to be undertaken around these issues, but one thing is clear—labelling everything "porn" is not helping.

> *"Human tragedies need to be dealt with and discussed with compassion, dignity, and sensitivity in a way that makes audiences more knowledgeable instead of arousing prurient interests in other people's suffering."*

Graphic Coverage of Disasters Can Generate Aid but Should Be Respectful of Victims

Stacey Patton

In the following viewpoint, the author maintains that graphic coverage of natural disasters, such as the images of dead bodies in New Orleans after Hurricane Katrina in 2005 and the massive earthquake in Haiti in 2010, are problematic. In one sense, there is an exploitative nature to graphic coverage that, she says, treats "all human misery like pornography." However, in another sense, she contends, these shocking images evoke an instinct in viewers to help the victims any way that they can. She argues that if such scenes were not broadcast, the outpouring of aid to Haiti and New Orleans may not have been so great. Nevertheless, she concludes that the news media must be very sensitive with its coverage, show-

ing respect for victims. Stacey Patton is a writer for the NAACP Legal Defense and Educational Fund.

As you read, consider the following questions:
1. How many Haitians does Patton report were killed in the 2010 earthquake?
2. Why does the author think that the actual number of bodies recovered after the Japanese earthquake has been so few?
3. According to the *New York Times*, as cited by Patton, what was the mass public response to the disaster in Japan in terms of mobilization of aid?

The American media treats all human misery like pornography.

There is a perversely titillating quality to the ways in which the news media exploits tragedies for their shock value without showing compassion for the victims. This is especially true of catastrophic events, be they manmade or natural disasters that strike the lives of people of color around the world.

The Lessons from Japan

But the ongoing news coverage of the recent earthquake and tsunami in Japan appears to be the exception.

On social media sites and blogs the conversations about the issue of showing dead bodies take their usual spin. Some say dead bodies should not be filmed out of respect for the dead and their families. Others say that the American media displays a racialist double standard of showing dead blacks and other foreigners of color while not graphically depicting the suffering and deaths of white bodies. I think the issues, especially as it relates to the disaster in Japan, are much more complex.

Unlike the disasters in Haiti, New Orleans, and Myanmar, we are not seeing Japan's dead. The incessant media images of gloom and doom, and death and degradation in the aftermath of the Katrina Hurricane in 2005, the cyclone that struck Myanmar in 2008, and the January 2010 earthquake that killed an estimated 200,000 Haitians, illustrates my point.

A Pattern of Graphic Images

Helicopter images from Myanmar showed us the horrific site of the half-clad uncollected and unburied bodies strewn across beaches. Muddied bodies were shown tangled in river branches alongside animal carcasses.

Dispatches from New Orleans brought us horrific videos and photos of bloated black bodies floating in murky soups of other black bodies, cars, animals, rooftops and other debris. I can't forget that infamous CNN clip of an elderly man who had died in his wheelchair in the sweltering heat while waiting outside the Louisiana Superdome for our government to respond.

From Port-au-Prince [Haiti] we were bombarded with scenes of looting and chaos. Images of the dead and dying scattered here and there were fed to the world for days on end. There were the photos of trucks piled with corpses. Black feet, arms and hands hung out of cracks of concrete rubble. Cameras captured bloodied, ashen, and naked babies and children lined next to each other like pickaninnies. There were those heartless displays of hundreds of dead men and women piled outside the morgue, their limbs in rigor mortis.

We saw shell-shocked Haitians covering their noses with makeshift masks in an attempt to mask the stench of death and decay. There were reports of animals eating corpses, mass burials, and crypts pried open, and the unceremonious disposal of bodies.

However, I will credit the media for documenting the government inefficiency in administering aid to the Haitian people and New Orleans residents. We did not see relief assistance given in a dignified manner that did not compromise

Graphic Images and Aid Money

From the *Miami Herald* to the *Palm Beach Post*, the *Birmingham News* to the *San Jose Mercury News*, the *Los Angeles Times* to the *Lincoln Journal Star*, the *New York Times* and more, the verdict was the same. Unvarnished stories and images of Haiti's horrific loss and the rare, miraculous rescue of victims dominated A sections and front page real estate for several days—in some cases, a week to 10 days and more. Many journalistic boundaries were crossed on television. CNN's Sanjay Gupta, a neurosurgeon, was photographed performing brain surgery on an injured Haitian girl; Anderson Cooper of the same network interrupted his on-the-scene newscast to sweep up a boy in the midst of a violent looting incident. Other newscasters were filmed giving water to the trapped and weeping.

The more images of unimaginable suffering were published, the more international aid poured in.

Arielle Emmett, "Too Graphic?," American Journalism Review, *March 2010.*

their safety and wellbeing. Proper steps to organize the distribution of aid to minimize the risk of riots and fighting among recipients were deplorable. The relief did not enable the victims to regain a sense of control following their overwhelming experiences.

A Different Picture in Japan

What we have been seeing from Japan is a different picture. Are the Japanese authorities not allowing their dead to be photographed and filmed out of respect for the victims? Is there some self-censorship happening from within the culture itself? How many of the dead are actually "visible," given that relatively few bodies were found in the first days after the quake and tsunami? Or, could it be that the U.S. media has chosen not to show such gruesome visuals because Japan is a modern, highly-developed society like ours?

As the nuclear crisis worsens, the media has emphasized the resilience, patience and orderliness of the Japanese people as they deal with the disruption, stress and emotional grief of this disaster. We've been told that tides of dead bodies have washed up in various places and have overwhelmed crematoriums.

We don't see looting. We don't see visible signs of anger. And we don't see their dead.

The tsunami apparently dragged many people out to sea and many others were buried in fields of debris that the water piled up. In addition, the threat of nuclear disaster has, in effect, overshadowed the other aftereffects of the disaster in part because the northern reaches of the country have been made so inaccessible and because relatively few bodies have yet been found. The actual number of bodies recovered yet is still low, even as officials say tens of thousands of people are still missing—many of them may be still out in the ocean.

Racial Aspects of Coverage

Still, if it is the case that the Japanese are not allowing the dead to be photographed or filmed, I'm wondering why leaders in the black world don't demand the same kind of respect and sanctuary for the dead. There seems to be a double standard in the ways in which the media deals with mass deaths of white versus people of color.

But what if black leaders around the world said "you can't film our dead?" How would that actually play with the rest of humanity?

One could argue that showing the suffering in graphic terms is not only a matter of exploitation on the part of television, but that it also provokes on the part of many viewers the "connection" that stimulates the desire and movement to help. The massive public response to Katrina—from whites, blacks and foreigners—was extraordinary. New Orleans in the wake of Katrina received more aid than any place else in the Gulf—be it Mobile or Biloxi because the devastation was greater and because it was much more visible. That was clearly a response to the visuals of the extraordinary, shocking scenes that television brought us.

The same can be said for Haiti. Think of all the medical people who rushed to [the] island nation because the television news had shown the need of the survivors for medical help. Within a day, the mass private mobilization had begun. The *New York Times* reported that the mass public response to the disaster in Japan, in terms of mobilization of aid, has been starkly muted.

If those scenes had been "hidden," not televised, the outpouring of aid from within and outside the U.S. to Katrina survivors and to Haitian survivors may not have been as great. Perhaps it was the pictures of the dead and the suffering of the survivors that provokes the outpouring of aid to the wounded.

A Thorny Issue

If in fact the Japanese have specified that they don't want their dead to be filmed or photographed, I commend them for respecting the final dignity that should be accorded in death. Here in America the question of showing dead bodies in the news has long been a controversial one and a double standard only when it comes to the dignity of dead white people. The Oklahoma City bombing, the World Trade Centers attack on Sept. 11, 2001, and the deaths of U.S. service personnel in the wars in Iraq and Afghanistan all forced journalists to grapple with this issue.

During rescue and recovery efforts in the aftermath of Katrina, FEMA [Federal Emergency Management Agency] requested that news organizations stop showing dead bodies as part of their coverage. Similar complaints were made against CNN by voices in the Caribbean who expressed concern for the dignity of the deceased and their families.

Facing criticism and accusations that FEMA was trying to censor or minimize the visual impact of the tragedy, the spokesperson for the federal agency acknowledged that decisions about such coverage lie with news editors, not government officials.

Nevertheless, the news media must understand that as they gather news about the human toll, they are also chronicling and writing the first draft of history. The words and images that get reported will provide a powerful testimony to the truths of tragedy. Yes, one of those unfortunate truths is the loss of life. I'm sure it is an ethical struggle for journalists and photographers to responsibly and respectfully gather information and pictures that memorialize such events.

I have to ask however, what is the point of showing the suffering and deaths of certain kinds of people and not others? What is the purpose of showing such images? What are the consequences of depicting death and what truths will such images help us understand?

Human tragedies need to be dealt with and discussed with compassion, dignity, and sensitivity in a way that makes audiences more knowledgeable instead of arousing prurient interests in other people's suffering. Perhaps we can learn a very important lesson from Japan.

*"Is this a journalist with loyalties to
journalism principles? Or this is a
physician with loyalties to his/her
medical professional oath? It is difficult
to be both."*

Physician Reporters Covering Disaster Zones Raises Serious Ethical Questions

Gary Schwitzer

In the following viewpoint, the author claims that a number of concerns have emerged about the role of physician-reporters in Haiti. With an increasing number of physicians functioning as journalists in disaster zones, he reports, critics contend that much of coverage seems like self-promotion and exploits the suffering of victims for public relations purposes. He employs the Potter Box, an ethical tool, in the situation and finds it is a complicated ethical issue that needs to be thoroughly discussed by physician-reporters and their news organizations in order to ensure that they are on the same page when the time comes to provide media coverage. Gary Schwitzer is publisher of the website HealthNewsReview.

As you read, consider the following questions:

1. Who was the Potter Box named after, according to Schwitzer?
2. According to the author, what does Bob Steele always ask journalists in his media workshops?
3. When does Schwitzer believe that journalism ethics discussions need to take place when it comes to physicians reporting from disaster zones?

I know that some people may not see any ethical conflict in physician-reporters like CNN's Sanjay Gupta, CBS's Jennifer Ashton and ABC's Richard Besser reporting on their own delivery of health care in Haiti.

But people who think a lot about these issues DO have concerns.

Journalism Ethics

Media ethics guru Bob Steele of the Poynter Institute and DePauw University told the *Los Angeles Times*: "It clouds the lens in terms of the independent observation and reporting." Given that Gupta's story involved a child who—in the end had a cut but no head injury—Steele said, "Frankly, it isn't much of a story. You can't help but look at this and worry there is a marketing element in it." *Los Angeles Times* media columnist James Rainey referred to it as "self-promotion." That's from a journalism ethics perspective.

Physician-ethicist Steve Miles, MD, of the University of Minnesota [UMN] Center for Bioethics wrote to me: "The reporters who have been practicing well-televised drive-by medical care in Haiti are demonstrating an appalling abuse of medical and journalistic ethics." He feels the decisions on what to broadcast are based on what presents itself as a "telegenic case."

Miles served as medical director for the American Refugee Committee for 25 years, including service as chief medical officer for 45,000 refugees on the Thai-Cambodian border and projects in Sudan, Croatia, Bosnia-Herzogovina, Indonesia, and the Thai-Burmese border. He is on the Board of the Center for Victims of Torture. He wrote:

> They justify this form of self-aggrandizement by its effect in mobilizing response for the larger disaster. The added value of their self promotion largely goes unchallenged.

Dr. Carl Elliott, also on the faculty of the UMN Center for Bioethics, wrote to me:

> It's worse than self-promotion. It's exploiting the suffering of Haitians for the PR [public relations] goals of their employers. They should not be reporting on their own work. That's a classic PR tactic: using humanitarian aid as a public relations device, in order to drive up ratings for their network.

The Potter Box

Allow me to drop back and apply an ethics tool to the situation. For years I've trained undergraduate journalism students in the use of the Potter Box, named after Ralph Potter, an emeritus professor of social ethics at Harvard Divinity School.

The box has four quadrants, which you can step through in this fashion.

Facts	Loyalties
Values	Principles

The facts of the situation are that these MD-reporters are in Haiti where there are overwhelming health care needs.

What are the different values at play? Clearly, the moral value of helping a person in need is a dominant value.

What ethical principles may apply to the situation? Again, the "persons as ends" or "do unto others" principle could dominate the decision-making. But Aristotle's or Confucius' golden mean might call for a middle ground of practical wisdom—an appropriate decision between two extremes. So, rather than doing nothing to help, or—at the other extreme—rather than reporting on one's own involvement in helping, a middle ground might be to help—but with the cameras off. In his media ethics workshops, Bob Steele always asks journalists to think about alternative pathways for telling a story—alternatives that might eliminate or minimize ethical conflicts.

To whom does the journalist have loyalties? This is probably the most essential quadrant of the Potter Box in this situation. Is this a journalist with loyalties to journalism principles? Or this is a physician with loyalties to his/her medical professional oath? It is difficult to be both. Time-honored journalism principles would dictate that a journalist should not be part of the story, that the "lens of independent observation and reporting" might be clouded if the reporter becomes part of the story. If an MD-reporter is guided by his/her sense of physician responsibility to care, look at how one citizen observer commented on the *LA Times* blog:

> With people dying around him every minute, he should not waste a single minute serving as a reporter. He's a doctor and it seems unethical to me that he is not spending every waking moment of his time providing medical care to the thousands that desperately need it. Can't CNN find any other reporters and spare him for a few weeks so he can save some lives? I appreciate the fact that he helped that baby, but he could help SO many more if he would just put down his microphone.

One could apply both the "values" and the "loyalties" questions to the news value of the stories. Why, exactly, were these episodes that Gupta, Ashton and Besser featured in, deemed to be newsworthy? Because they were outstanding news stories? Or because it was a way to feature a CNN, CBS, or ABC employee in an active, care-giving role?

The code of ethics of the Radio-Television News Directors Association states: "Resist any self-interest or peer pressure that might erode journalistic duty and service to the public."

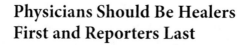

Physicians Should Be Healers First and Reporters Last

If reporters who are also physicians want so badly to step out of their journalistic role to help, [Dr. Steven Miles, of the University of Minnesota Center for Bioethics] argues, they should volunteer instead with relief agencies in Haiti—and set aside an hour a day to grant interviews to their network employers.

David Folkenflik, "Reporters Who Are MDs Find Lines Blurred in Haiti," National Public Radio, January 20, 2010. www.npr.org.

An Ethical Dilemma

The Potter Box demonstrates the complexity of the ethical decision-making involved. The first two quadrants might seem like a slam-dunk in favor of the MD-reporters doing whatever they could to lend a hand of help. But the last two quadrants raise considerable complexities.

So the comments that media ethicist Bob Steele and media columnist James Rainey made were not just trivial comments made by people in the Ivory Tower or sitting on the sidelines of journalism—as I've seen some online comments charge. They raise legitimate journalism ethics concerns which are worthy of greater thought and consideration.

Before getting on a plane to Haiti, each of these MD-reporters and their news organizations knew what they were getting into. Such journalism ethics discussions need to take place in newsrooms before events take place—not during or after. What discussions took place? Or was it a matter of: "Go down there. Jump into action as soon as you can and we'll put it on the air?"

Ivan Oransky, a journalist who earned his MD, responded to my request for a reaction:

> When you're the only specialist—or even doctor—around for miles, treating victims of wars and natural disasters you come across is the natural human inclination. I actually think it's both understandable and justifiable, and probably even commendable.
>
> But where these episodes start to worry me is when networks start making their doctors' heroics into the story, and then pound viewers with clips repeatedly. That's what all the networks are doing now. What I'm not in favor of is the reporter becoming the story, and the episode turning into marketing. It smacks of all kinds of exploitation, and it throws independence and skepticism into serious question. There are already enough forces eroding those principles.

"When you could see photo captions of white Hurricane Katrina survivors side-by-side with black survivors, the racial double standards in the news media covering a catastrophic event were obvious."

Natural Disaster Coverage Displays Widespread Racial Biases

Natalie Hopkinson

In the following viewpoint, a writer contends that a recent picture in the New York Times *of a young Haitian boy running with a white plastic bag symbolizes the widespread racial biases in disaster coverage. She argues that the media tend to treat the races differently when it comes to disaster coverage: blacks are often portrayed as menacing and lawless; whites are described as doing what they need to do to survive. Another racial element in disaster coverage, the author maintains, is the demeaning idea that Haiti and New Orleans were cursed and that the displacement of black residents is referred to by the media as a refugee situation. Natalie Hopkinson is the website* The Root's *media and culture critic.*

As you read, consider the following questions:

1. According to the author, what political strategist and New Orleans native drew facile parallels between the disasters in Haiti and New Orleans?
2. According to Kathleen Parker, as cited by Hopkinson, what is the source of the urban legend that the devil cursed Haiti?
3. What was the horrific incident told to reporters Simon Romero and Marc Lacey that the author believes may not be completely true?

An arresting Damon Winter photo of a Haitian child graces the cover of the Sunday *New York Times*. A boy of about 10 wearing a bright red, oversized Polo shirt is caught mid-stride by the camera, dashing through the streets of Port-au-Prince, eyes gazing purposely ahead, gripping a white plastic bag.

The caption gives a seemingly "objective" recitation of the facts. "Haitians fled gunshots that rang out in downtown Port-au-Prince Saturday. Tons of relief supplies had arrived for delivery." It is up to the viewer to connect the dots, and connect them to another front-page article below the fold: "Looting Flares Where Order Breaks Down."

So was the kid looting?

The Racial Double Standard

Nearly five years ago, when you could see photo captions of white Hurricane Katrina survivors side-by-side with black survivors, the racial double standards in the news media covering a catastrophic tragedy were obvious. Hungry, desperate white survivors were "finding food" while hungry, desperate black survivors were "looting" for food.

Since the earthquake hit Haiti, I don't know what is more troubling: That so many observers, including political strategist and New Orleans native Donna Brazile, have been drawing facile parallels between the two cities, or that so many of those comparisons are turning out to be true.

Start with this "the devil" cursed Port-au-Prince business. I discussed the truth about how Haitians managed to defeat the French army, without a Satanic assist in this essay. And Kathleen Parker uncovered the source of this urban legend (turns out it was a 1791 voodoo ceremony).

But this devil talk also came up in the wake of Katrina. Another so-called Christian, Pastor John Hagee, one of John McCain's high-profile backers, told NPR's Terry Gross that Hurricane Katrina was, in fact, the judgment of God against the city of New Orleans. "New Orleans had a level of sin that was offensive to God," Hagee said, because "there was to be a homosexual parade there on the Monday that Katrina came."

Graphic Images Abound

Philip Kennicott of the *Washington Post* believes that Hurricane Katrina helped pave the way for loosening standards for how graphic images can be published in the news media. He calls the graphic nature of the images coming out of Port-au-Prince dehumanizing. "Bodies caked in dust and plaster, faces covered in blood, the dead stacked in the streets without sheets to hide them—these are all violations of the unwritten code [how] death can only be seen, in the established etiquette of the mainstream media," he wrote in a recent essay.

> [Haiti] was a country tossed aside, seemingly consigned to the status of a street person whose needs are intractable . . . The camera is recording something elemental that will affect everything to do with the future of this troubled country. It is asking if these are people, like us. It is asking if we believe they are human.

I am inclined to find the Port-au-Prince images so far more illuminating than exploitive. But Kennicott's larger point about the way the camera views brown people is totally sound. The lynching scene depicted in the Sunday *New York Times* was appalling. It is one thing to "find" bread; it is quite another to break into stores and score bolts of carpet and luggage while intimidating people with machetes and guns.

Eyewitnesses told the journalists Simon Romero and Marc Lacey that police yanked a man accused of looting off a truck, and watched as he was beaten to death, and set afire by an angry mob. Since there is no photographic evidence and the reporters reported the scene second-hand, it is hard to know with 100 percent certainty that this happened.

But what is 100 percent true is that that awful scene had nothing to do with the child in the red shirt whose photo was snapped as food and supplies were being given away. In general, that photo conjures an image of black anarchy, aka The Horror.

Katrina and the Haiti Earthquake

Maybe most telling when it comes to parallels between Katrina and the Haiti earthquake is the debate over what to call the displaced people. In the first days following Katrina, news outlets, big and small were calling the American citizens displaced by the hurricane "refugees."

I was teaching journalism to university undergraduates at the time, and one of my students vigorously defended using the word "refugee" in that context. When pressed for a definition of "refugee," which Webster's called "a person who flees to a foreign country or power to escape danger or persecution," he held firm. "They are refugees. I watch CNN; I know what they look like."

The confusion is worth remembering in the coming months and years, when there will be actual refugees coming to the United States' shores. They will be brown. They will poor. They will be desperate.

Whatever we call them, the media images of them will tell a truth of their own.

Periodical and Internet Sources Bibliography

The following articles have been chosen to supplement the diverse views presented in this chapter.

Mario Almonte — "The Wild Ones: Are American Journalists Reckless, Oblivious or Brave?," *Huffington Post*, April 26, 2011. www.huffingtonpost.com.

Jo Chandler — "Media's Crimes of Omission Leaves Disaster Victims in the Lurch," *Sydney Morning Herald*, September 17, 2010.

Lyndal Curtis — "Disasters and the Media: A Necessary Voice," *The Drum*, February 24, 2011. www.abc.net.au.

Arielle Emmett — "Too Graphic?," *American Journalism Review*, March 2010.

Arya Gunawan — "Media's Role in Times of Natural Disasters," *Jakarta Post* (Indonesia), June 3, 2011.

Amrita Jayakumar — "Choices in Crises," Global Journalist, September 1, 2011. www.globaljournalist.org.

Dan Murphy — "Haiti Earthquake: Is the Term 'Looting' Racist? Past Kanye West Comments Fuel Debate," *Christian Science Monitor*, January 19, 2010.

Natalie Savino — "Disaster Coverage: When Is Enough Enough?," *Punch*, February 25, 2011.

Noam Scheiber — "The Disaster Pool," *New Republic*, January 19, 2010.

Todd A. Smith — "Recent Natural Disasters Shouldn't Make Us Forget Katrina," *Real Black Men's Magazine*, March 17, 2011.

Rebecca Solnit — "When the Media Is the Disaster: Covering Haiti," *Huffington Post*, January 21, 2010. www.huffingtonpost.com.

For Further Discussion

Chapter 1

1. The link between global warming and natural disasters is a controversial topic in the United States. Brad Plumer contends that global warming increases the frequency and severity of natural disasters. Rich Trzupek suggests that that link has been disproved. After reading both viewpoints, outline your opinion on the debate. How do you perceive the link between global warming and natural disasters? Cite from the viewpoints in your answer.

2. Stephanie Pappas argues that many Americans believe God plays a significant role in natural disasters, while Eric Marrapodi posits that they look for other explanations. Whose argument do you find more compelling? What role does religion play in the response to and understanding of natural disasters?

Chapter 2

1. Saundra Schimmelpfennig suggests that the way that charities raise money in response to natural disasters does not work. Do you agree or disagree with her suggestions on how to fix the system? Why or why not? Do you see other solutions to the problems with aid organizations today? What are they?

2. In the aftermath of the Haitian earthquake, many critics maintain that humanitarian aid to the country has only exacerbated problems such as corruption, violence, and poverty. Ian Birrell is one of those voices. What role has disaster relief played in Haiti? How can the process of humanitarian aid be improved?

Chapter 3

1. Christian Parenti contends that the federal government should be responsible for disaster relief. Matt Mayer,

David C. John, and James Jay Carafano maintain that the states should have primary responsibility. Bruce Walker argues that it should be private charities. Which viewpoint is most persuasive and why?

2. Does the Federal Emergency Management Agency effectively coordinate disaster relief and services? Read the viewpoints by FEMA and Ron Paul to inform your answer. Is FEMA essential to disaster relief efforts, or should it be? Explain.

3. Militarized aid has been a hot topic in international aid circles. James L. Schoff and Marina Travayiakis suggest that there are advantages to this approach. Jamie Way argues that militarized aid holds too many dangers. In your opinion, should militarized aid be utilized in the aftermath of natural disasters? Why or why not?

Chapter 4

1. In his viewpoint, Patrick Cockburn characterizes the media coverage of natural disasters as superficial and misleading. Simon Moss calls it formulaic and a detriment to aid efforts. David Sirota argues that it resembles pornography. Natalie Hopkinson detects a widespread racial bias to media reports. Which criticism do you feel is the most persuasive and why? Which is the most difficult to address? Explain.

2. The viewpoints in this chapter explore the media coverage of natural disasters. Several viewpoints criticize the coverage, others defend the sensationalism of the media for generating sympathy and donations. Which viewpoint best encapsulates your opinion on the subject of media coverage? Explain why.

3. One recent controversy in the media coverage of natural disasters is the role of physicians in disaster zones. Gary Schwitzer outlines some of the ethical questions raised by media critics. What do you believe should be the role of physicians in media coverage of disasters?

Organizations to Contact

The editors have compiled the following list of organizations concerned with the issues debated in this book. The descriptions are derived from materials provided by the organizations. All have publications or information available for interested readers. The list was compiled on the date of publication of the present volume; names, addresses, phone and fax numbers, and e-mail and Internet addresses may change. Be aware that many organizations take several weeks or longer to respond to inquiries, so allow as much time as possible.

American Red Cross
2025 E St. NW
Washington, DC 20006
(202) 303-4498
website: www.redcross.org

The American Red Cross was established in 1881 to provide humanitarian care and aid to the victims of war, terrorist attacks, and natural disasters. It offers domestic disaster relief, community services for the needy, and support for military families. The American Red Cross also runs blood donation drives and educational programs on the subject of health and safety. The organization helps millions of Americans every year. Its website features information on recent domestic and international humanitarian efforts, including the Japanese earthquake and tsunami. It also has a photo and video library, press releases, and ways to contribute or volunteer in your area.

Centers for Disease Control and Prevention (CDC)
1600 Clifton Rd.
Atlanta, GA 30333
(800) 232-4636
e-mail: cdcinfo@cdc.gov
website: www.cdc.gov

The Centers for Disease Control and Prevention is the US government agency responsible for monitoring the nation's health and investigating health problems and disease outbreaks. The CDC also works to develop and implement sound health policies, which derive from comprehensive research, surveys, and collaboration with local, regional, and national partners. The CDC promotes healthy behaviors and emphasizes disease prevention. In the case of a natural disaster, the CDC would be on the ground working with local authorities, the Department of Health and Human Services, and the Federal Emergency Management Agency (FEMA) to safeguard health and health systems and deal with any disease outbreak in the aftermath. The CDC website features vital information on the agency's work, including podcasts and blogs that cover recent initiatives and activities. It also offers access to a range of publications, including the *Emerging Infectious Diseases Journal* and the *Morbidity and Mortality Weekly Report*.

Central Intelligence Agency (CIA)
Office of Public Affairs
Washington, DC 20505
(703) 482-0623 • fax: (703) 482-1739
website: www.cia.gov

Established in 1947, the Central Intelligence Agency is the civilian intelligence agency of the US government. It is responsible for gathering intelligence on foreign governments and terrorist organizations and provides national security assessments to US policy makers. The CIA's intelligence-gathering activities range from assessing emerging and existing threats to the US government, monitoring and analyzing correspondence and Internet communications, implementing tactical operations in foreign countries, developing and managing intelligence assets, and launching counterterrorism efforts, to dealing with threats to the US computer systems. A major role of the CIA is to find information on terrorist threats to the United States, including those that may try to take advantage of natural disasters. The CIA website offers a featured story archive, recent press releases and statements, speeches and testimony by CIA officials, and a page for kids to learn about CIA initiatives.

Department of Health and Human Services (HHS)
200 Independence Ave. SW
Washington, DC 20201
(877) 696-6775
website: www.hhs.gov

The Department of Health and Human Services is the US government agency in charge of protecting the health of and providing essential health services to all Americans. HHS works closely with state and local governments to develop programs and implement policies. The HHS also promotes healthy behaviors and emphasizes disease prevention. In the case of a natural disaster, the HHS would work with local authorities, the Centers for Disease Control and Prevention, and the Federal Emergency Management Agency to safeguard health and health systems and deal with any disease outbreak in the aftermath. The HHS website offers a series of fact sheets as well as other educational information.

Department of Homeland Security (DHS)
Twelfth and C Sts. SW
Washington, DC 20024
(202) 282-8000
website: www.dhs.gov

The Department of Homeland Security is tasked with protecting the United States from terrorist attacks and other threats. Established after the terrorist attacks of September 11, 2001, the DHS aims to reduce the vulnerability of US infrastructure and installations, government officials, and major events to attacks of any kind; to enforce and administer immigration laws to better control who is traveling in and out of the country; to coordinate and administer the national response to terrorist attacks and be a key player in recovery and rebuilding efforts; and to safeguard and secure cyberspace by assessing cyberthreats and coordinating a counterattack. The DHS works closely with other government agencies and relevant partners to protect the nation in the aftermath of natural disasters. It oversees the Federal Emergency Management Agency, which supports "citizens and first responders to ensure that as a nation we work together to build, sustain, and improve our capability to prepare for, protect against, respond to, recover from, and mitigate all hazards." The DHS website allows access to a number of informative resources, including fact sheets, breaking news, press releases, speeches and testimony of DHS officials, videos, and other publications on topics of interest.

Department of State
2201 C St. NW
Washington, DC 20520
(202) 647-4000
website: www.state.gov

The Department of State is the federal agency that is responsible for formulating, implementing, and assessing US foreign policy. The State Department also assists US citizens living or traveling abroad; promotes and protects US business interests all over the world; and support the activities of other US agencies in foreign countries. The State Department is active in enacting diplomatic efforts and informing Congress, the president, and the public about the political, economic, and social events related to foreign policy. It also oversees the Bureau of Counterterrorism (CT), which is focused on developing coordinated strategies to defeat terrorists abroad and in advancing the counterterrorism objectives of the United States. The State Department website features a wealth of information on current policies, upcoming events, daily schedules of top officials, and updates from various countries. It also has videos, congressional testimony, speech transcripts, background notes, human rights reports, and strategy reviews.

Federal Aviation Agency (FAA)

800 Independence Ave. SW
Washington, DC 20591
(866) TELL-FAA
website: www.faa.gov

The Federal Aviation Agency is the US federal agency tasked with overseeing and regulating the nation's aviation industry. As an agency of the US Department of Transportation, the FAA regulates commercial airline transportation; develops and operates the air traffic control system; creates and enforces flight inspection standards; facilitates new aerospace technology and safety regulations; and investigates airplane crashes, accidents, and other aviation incidents. Another of the FAA's responsibilities is to conduct research on the nation's commercial and general aviation safety record, which can be found on the FAA website. The agency also provides access to airport compliance records, air traffic information and guidelines, recent testimony from FAA officials, fact sheets and statistics, training resources and manuals, and regulatory information.

Federal Emergency Management Agency (FEMA)

500 C St. SW
Washington, DC 20472
(202) 646-2500
website: www.fema.gov

According to the mission statement of the Federal Emergency Management Agency, the agency supports "citizens and first responders to ensure that as a nation we work together to build, sustain, and improve our capability to prepare for, protect against, respond to, recover from, and mitigate all hazards." To accomplish this, FEMA works with federal partners, state, and local governments, tribal officials, large and small businesses, nonprofit organizations, and the general public. It has developed the National Response Framework, a comprehensive approach to all kinds of domestic incidents, particularly national disasters. The National Response Framework can be accessed on the FEMA website, which also offers a wealth of information on the agency's activities, recent natural disasters, and the types of assistance available for victims of a natural disaster.

National Emergency Response Team (NERT)
1058 Albion Rd.
Unity, ME 04988
(207) 948-3499 • fax: (207) 948-3505
e-mail: contactus@nert-usa.org
website: www.nert-usa.org

The National Emergency Response Team was established in 1993 to "conceive, develop and implement disaster response services and educational programs that coordinate publicly available resources during a crisis situation." NERT is staffed by volunteers, many with experience in the transportation and disaster relief field, who mobilize during and after natural crises to procure needed materials—clothes, equipment, and temporary shelter—and deliver it to where it is most needed. NERT also offers training and community education programs.

Natural Disasters Association
e-mail: info@n-d-a.org
website: www.n-d-a.org

The Natural Disasters Association is dedicated to educating the public on national disasters, preparedness, and disaster relief. It oversees the Natural Disasters website, which offers a breakdown of natural hazards by type; for example, there are sections on tsunamis, hurricanes, landslides, pestilence, and a number of others. The website also features a forum in which users can discuss topics related to natural disasters all over the world and a blog that covers breaking news and ongoing efforts regarding catastrophic events and natural disasters.

Bibliography of Books

Daniel P. Aldrich — *Building Resilience: Social Capital in Post-disaster Recovery.* Chicago: University of Chicago Press, 2012.

Judy L. Baker, ed. — *Climate Change, Disaster Risk, and the Urban Poor: Cities Building Resilience for a Changing World.* Washington, DC: World Bank, 2012.

Virginia M. Brennan, ed. — *Natural Disasters and Public Health: Hurricanes Katrina, Rita, and Wilma.* Baltimore: Johns Hopkins University Press, 2009.

Sara E. Davis and Luke Glanville, eds. — *Protecting the Displaced: Deepening the Responsibility to Protect.* Boston: Martinus Nijhoff, 2010.

Bruce A. Elleman — *Waves of Hope: The US Navy's Response to the Tsunami in Northern Indonesia.* Newport, RI: Naval War College Press, 2007.

Terence E. Fretheim — *Creation Untamed: The Bible, God, and Natural Disasters.* Grand Rapids, MI: Baker Academic, 2010.

Kathryn Gow, ed. — *Meltdown: Climate Change, Natural Disasters, and Other Catastrophes—Fears and Concerns of the Future.* Hauppauge, NY: Nova Science, 2009.

John Hannigan — *Disasters Without Borders.* Boston: Polity, 2012.

William Hayes — *What Went Wrong: Investing the Worst Man-Made and Natural Disasters.* New York: Hearst Books, 2011.

Stefan Kiesbye, ed. — *Are Natural Disasters Increasing?* Detroit: Greenhaven Press, 2010.

Scott Gabriel Knowles — *The Disaster Experts: Mastering Risk in Modern America.* Philadelphia: University of Pennsylvania Press, 2011.

Andrew Lakoff, ed. — *Disaster and the Politics of Intervention.* New York: Columbia University Press, 2010.

Erwin W. Lutzer — *An Act of God? Answers to Tough Questions About God's Role in Natural Disasters.* Carol Stream, IL: Tyndale House, 2011.

Charles Officer and Jake Page, eds. — *When the Planet Rages: Natural Disasters, Global Warming, and the Future of the Earth.* New York: Oxford University Press, 2009.

Christian Parenti — *Tropic of Chaos: Climate Change and the New Geography of Violence.* New York: Nation Books, 2011.

Mark Pelling — *Adaptation to Climate Change.* New York: Routledge, 2010.

Charles Perrow — *The Next Catastrophe: Reducing Our Vulnerabilities to Natural, Industrial, and Terrorist Disasters.* Princeton, NJ: Princeton University Press, 2007.

Linda Polman — *The Crisis Caravan: What's Wrong with Humanitarian Aid?* New York: Metropolitan Books, 2010.

Anouk Ride and Diane Bretherton — *Community Resilience in Natural Disasters.* New York: Palgrave Macmillan, 2011.

Amanda Ripley — *The Unthinkable: Who Survives When Disaster Strikes and Why.* New York: Crown, 2008.

Matthew R. Stein — *When Technology Fails: A Manual for Self-Reliance, Sustainability, and Surviving the Long Emergency.* Rev. ed. White River Junction, VT: Chelsea Green, 2008.

Gary Stern — *Can God Intervene? How Religion Explains Natural Disasters.* Westport, CT: Praeger, 2007.

Henrik Svensen — *The End Is Nigh: A History of Natural Disasters.* London: Reaktion, 2009.

David K. Twigg — *The Politics of Disaster: Tracking the Impact of Hurricane Andrew.* Gainesville: University Press of Florida, 2012.

Christian Webersik   *Climate Change and Security: A Gathering Storm of Global Challenges.* Santa Barbara, CA: Praeger, 2010.

Index

CPSIA information can be obtained
at www.ICGtesting.com
Printed in the USA
FFOW020910110213
860FF